The Roads We Traveled

Hiram Maxim nervously wheeled out his home-made motorized bicycle one morning in 1894. He carefully pushed it up a hill, straddled the seat, and began a descent that propelled him with explosions, fire, and smoke at an unheard-of speed. Follow the escapades of the men who dared to motorize transportation from the invention of the steam engine in 1712 to the first transcontinental car races in America and wild Model T treks during the roaring twenties. This entertaining history tracks the triumphs and blunders of such notables as Ransom Olds, Henry Ford, and Louis Chevrolet. Meet the men whose creativity and determination helped put the world on wheels.

The Roads We Traveled

An Amusing History of the Automobile

Douglas Waitley

Photographs

JULIAN MESSNER
NEW YORK

Published by Julian Messner
A Simon & Schuster Division of
Gulf & Western Corporation
Simon & Schuster Building
1230 Avenue of the Americas
New York, New York 10020

Designed by Irving Perkins
Manufactured in the United States of America

Library of Congress Cataloging in Publication Data

Waitley, Douglas.
The roads we traveled.

Bibliography: p. 215
Includes index.
1. Automobile industry and trade—United
States—History. 2. Automobile racing—United
States—History. I. Title.
TL23.W27   629.2'0973   78–21082
ISBN 0–671–32911–1

Contents

The Roads We Traveled

1

The Wild Ride

It was a late summer night in 1892. The air was heady with the perfume of growing things. A young man on a bicycle pedaled along a quiet country road. He was a handsome lad with silky black hair and a fine, fashionable mustache. There was a look of extreme pleasure on his face, for he had just spent a most enjoyable evening with a lovely young lady from a neighboring town.

As Hiram Maxim pedaled slowly through the darkness, he had a strange vision. He thought that it would be a wonderful thing if a little engine was to be devised which would furnish the power to drive a bicycle. The creation of a little engine which would do what his legs were doing did not appear to pose a serious problem. He could not be expending more than a sixth or a quarter of a horsepower, and that would not mean much of an engine.

Hiram Maxim had in mind using a machine something like the recently invented Otto gasoline engine to power his bicycle. Soon after his night vision, Hiram examined one of the Otto engines. It was a relatively simple machine: just a cylinder with a piston inside. It received its power when small quantities of gas were ignited at regular intervals by a spark at the top of the cylinder. Hiram, a recent college graduate, felt that he should be able to adapt this type of engine to run a bicycle.

Hiram was an employee of the Thomson Electric Welding Company, so he already knew something about machinery. But he knew nothing about the fuel which ran the engine. It was called "gasoline" and had only recently been discovered as a by-product of oil distillation. Hiram's only experience with this gasoline-stuff was when he had used it to remove paint from his clothing. He realized he must find out more about gasoline's properties. He bought an eight-ounce jar of gasoline from the only store in town that sold it—the paint shop.

Maxim waited anxiously for his factory to close that day so he could experiment with his gasoline. Finally six o'clock came. When the building was deserted, he brought out the bottle. "It was a colorless, limpid, innocent-appearing liquid," he later wrote. "No one would ever suspect it to be loaded with epoch-making possibilities."

Hiram planned what he called a "get acquainted test." He poured a small amount of gasoline into a metal container. Then he put a wooden stopper in the top and rolled the gasoline around until it had vaporized. Feeling he now had an agreeable mixture of air and gas somewhat similar to that required by the gas pump engines, he removed the stopper and tossed in a lighted match.

There was a short, very tense pause. "Then the end of the world came, it seemed to me. There was a terrifying explosion; fire shot up out of the [container, which] staggered drunkenly on the bench; and the match I had thrown in went hurtling to the ceiling." Maxim stared, his mouth hanging open. He quickly concluded that there was roughly a thousand times more kick in a drop of gasoline than he had expected.

Now that Hiram had his fuel, all he needed was an engine and some vehicle to attach it to.

The vehicle was relatively easy, though very expensive. For the staggering sum of thirty dollars, he bought a second-hand tricycle with worn, solid-rubber tires and a dangerous tip to the right.

The engine was far more difficult. For the next year and a half he labored on its construction during almost all of his spare moments. Everything had to be done from scratch. Nowhere in the world was he able to purchase spark plugs that would stand a roadway's jostling—or a suitable carburetor. Nor were there any good batteries, or steering wheels, or gear combinations. This was the very beginning of the automotive era. "Every detail about the automobile," Maxim wrote, "had to be learned in the hard school of experience."

By late 1894 the engine was finally finished. It was a greasy, three-cylinder affair about a foot high and a foot wide. Before Hiram hooked it up to his tricycle, he decided to give it its first test while in the factory.

After the work day, Hiram's fellow employees gathered around to watch. They smiled, for they knew the odd contraption would not work. Hiram ran an electric line from a factory outlet to the engine distributor. This would send the "juice" to igniters in each of the three cylinder-heads at the proper moment for combustion. Then Hiram fastened a belt from a factory machine to the engine's crankshaft. The onlookers' grins became broader and they nudged each other in amusement.

Hiram planned that as the belt turned the crankshaft, the piston would descend, thereby sucking a gas-air mixture from the gas tank into the top of the cylinder. When the piston rose with the next crankcase stroke, an electric spark would cause the gas to ignite. This explosion would send the piston plunging downward without any help from Maxim. The engine would then continue the up-down cycle on its own.

Maxim imagined the machine would run smoothly and quietly. But he had had no experience with an unmuffled, three-cylinder engine!

The factory lathe turned the crankcase. Everyone was quiet.

Suddenly the engine caught. Then there was what Maxim thought was the roar of machine-gun fire:

> I had never heard such a terrible clatter. Noise came from everywhere. . . . We had no warning at all. Hell just broke loose and there we were right in the middle of it! . . . Every toolmaker scrambled to a position that suggested preparation for dodging flying missiles. Not a one of them ever had heard such an astonishing noise. . . . Blue smoke filled the room and curled out of the exhaust pipes of the little engine. . . . Here was the most savage, impetuous, noisy, and riotous little spitfire that the mind of man could conceive!

Maxim finally got the engine to stop by shutting off the plant's electric power. He was thoroughly shaken. "I have to confess," he wrote, "that I was afraid of the little engine, for it had given me a very bad fright. If it was going to go off like a bunch of cannon crackers every time I started it, there was not so much fun in fooling with it."

But Hiram soon recovered and dared place the engine on his tricycle in preparation for an actual road test.

Everything in his motorized vehicle was pretty much on a catch-as-catch-can basis. The chain which connected the engine with the rear wheels was a rusty part of the original trike. In place of a carburetor to mix the gas vapor with air, Maxim simply had a small kerosene can in which Mother Nature jostled the brew into something approaching the proper composition. The gas-air combination was led to the motor by a copper tube, probably picked up from his factory junk heap. The accelerator-throttle was a primitive valve set in the gas line that Maxim would have to adjust by hand while he bounced along the road. Maxim's electric system consisted of a few batteries similar to those used in ordinary flashlights!

One morning in the fall of 1894, Hiram nervously wheeled his motorcycle out of the factory closet where he had been keeping it. It was barely past dawn, so he hoped that no one in West Lynn, Massachusetts, would be up to see him possibly make a fool of himself in his crazy-appearing contraption.

Hiram pedaled down the driveway toward the street. It took him only a few seconds, however, to discover his first mistake. He had assumed that pedaling would crank the motor and start it. But this did not occur. Far from it—the drag of the engine pistons was so great that Hiram was thoroughly winded after weaving forward only a few yards. Puffing and exhausted, he sat glumly on the cycle. He realized that it would take nothing less than a team of plow horses to pull his blasted engine fast enough to start it!

He debated his course of action. What he needed was a clutch to disengage the engine from the chain that connected it to the rear axle. He also needed a crank to get the motor started. But he had neither of these. What could he do?

After much pondering, Hiram's face lit up. Using a large screwdriver, he pried the chain from its sprocket. Then, with

Hiram Maxim aboard his motor-driven cycle, 1895.

the motor disengaged, he pedaled the heavy tricycle toward
a hill. Once on the slope, he had to push the clumsy vehicle
up. It was tough work, with the gravel giving way beneath
his feet and the front wheel wobbling nearly out of control
through ruts. At last the summit was reached. Hiram then
replaced the chain and prepared to descend the hill, hoping he
could thereby get enough speed to start the stubborn engine.

Tensely he turned the ignition on. Then he adjusted the accelerator-throttle valve. Finally he clambered onto the seat and gingerly headed downward. Although he began to descend, the engine drag was so strong that the pace was hardly encouraging. Hiram frantically fussed with the accelerator, pushing it ever farther toward a rich gas mixture. Meanwhile the tricycle swerved from one side to another as the wheels caught the ruts. While Hiram juggled his attention between steering and playing with the accelerator, the trike bounced violently on its hard rubber tires. Hiram saw the bottom of the hill approaching. In a few seconds it would all be over: a complete failure.

He could think of no way to get his engine to start. He had given it all the gas possible. It was almost as if the devilish little thing were laughing at him. Half in anger, half in desperation, he shoved the accelerator lever over to the lean side. Then he got action—more than he had bargained for:

> . . . there came a terrific snapping noise and what seemed to be a rear-end collision. I firmly believed something big had . . . hit me in the rear. The tricycle gave a lunge ahead and started for the bottom of the hill hell-for-leather, regardless of loose stones, rocks, and gullies, at a speed that seemed nothing short of horrible. Careening, sliding, spouting loose stones, fire and smoke, it roared ahead. I had all I could do to keep aboard and steer. As for manipulating the throttle and mixture valves, I was many times too busy to think of such details.

With his feet up around his ears, Hiram had almost no control of his motorcycle. In a few seconds, however, he was able to steady himself somewhat. Just in time, too, for he was headed down a deep rut toward danger. He yanked his steering lever with such force that the rubber tire peeled right off the rim and snarled up in the wheel. With that, the wheel jammed and Hiram was sent flying through the air.

For a moment the inventor sat dazed on the ground. There was silence except for the spinning of the back wheels and the trickle of gasoline from his spiteful machine. Hiram rose shakily to his feet. He had several bad cuts and bruises, and his torn trousers would cause some problems when he returned home. But he was grateful, for such a fall could have really hurt him.

Hiram examined his motorcycle. Surprisingly, it was not as badly damaged as he had feared. With a little bending here and straightening there, he was able to get the front wheel to roll. With that he trudged back to the factory. But it was not a discouraging hike. Although his ten-second ride had been a long way from his dream of gliding smoothly through the countryside, his machine had actually worked!

Hiram knew he had a lot more tinkering to do. Yet it would just be a matter of time before he would be able to make a practical motor-propelled vehicle. He hummed happily as he began sketching a new engine model.

2

The Creation of
the Fabulous Buggyaut

Long before Hiram Maxim's rough-and-tumble ride, horse-less vehicles had been on people's minds. In fact, ever since the invention of the steam engine in 1712, radicals had been fussing with pistons and boiler plates in the attempt to conjure up some sort of contrivance that would turn carriage wheels. However, early steam boilers were so heavy that they posed severe problems for hopefuls wishing to make the world's first operable car.

There was, for example, the ambitious French artillery officer, Nicholas Cugnot, who in 1769 fitted a steam boiler four feet wide on scaffolding overhanging a wheeled platform. The odd thing actually moved under its own power. But Cugnot's elation promptly cooled as his lopsided car plowed into a wall. His next (and last) effort terminated with a smashing overturn on a Paris street corner while tearing along at the frightful speed of three miles per hour.

Although Cugnot's autos suffered quick finales, the idea did not die. By 1801, Richard Trevithick was road testing what he called the London Steam Carriage. The smoke-belching steam engine drove a series of huge gears attached to the carriage wheels. These gears were so large that riders had difficulty wiggling around them to reach their seats. The progress of this vehicle through the countryside was marked by a nerve-whanging snarl of engine parts. After Richard and his machine had lurched into the distance, the sooty engine left a grimy souvenir staining the landscape.

Despite their handicaps, around two dozen of Richard's bone-bruising vehicles eventually were livening English roads. As the decades passed, other steam-driven carriages began cutting through Britain. Such was their potential that the railroad lobby swung into action. By suspicious means, in 1865 Parliament was induced to pass the Red Flag Act. This law limited steam carriages to a lazy 4 mph in the country and a creeping 2 mph in towns. To add to the humiliation, every steam carriage had to be preceded by a man on foot carrying a red flag to warn travelers and their motor-shy horses that one of the hissing, smoking monstrosities was descending on them. For thirty-one years thereafter red-flag-men sauntered British highways keeping the speed of motoring within lawful limits and thereby destroying the budding British auto industry.

In France and Germany the attitude was more favorable. In 1873, Amedée Bellee produced a large coal-fired vehicle that carried up to twelve passengers. To ride in Bellee's auto, with its four rock-finding, iron-rimmed wheels, was more an ordeal than an exercise in transportation luxury. Not even the

French could love the lumbering creation which its inventor hopefully named L'Obeissante, or the Obedient One. As a result, the grotesque thing played no part in future automobile development.

Americans, too, were working on steam cars. In 1875, an inventor with the unlikely name of Carhart managed to drive a machine nearly two hundred miles from Green Bay, Wisconson, to Madison. He averaged a respectable twenty mph (faster than a trotting horse) over the rutted, unpaved roads. In 1886 Ransom Olds produced the steam-driven grandpaw of the Oldsmobile. It was a three-wheeler about which young Ransom quipped: "It never kicks or bites . . . and only eats while on the road." But steamers were not the answer to reliable highway travel, for they needed storage for too much water and coal, took too long to heat up for short runs, and were too closely associated in the public mind with heralded explosions on steamboats and railroad engines.

Much more promising than the dangerously pressurized steam boilers were the gasoline engines which, since the early 1880s, had been driving water pumps and motorboats, and performing duties in machine shops. As the gas engines became better and better known, it was only a matter of time before inventors with more savvy than Hiram Maxim learned how to adapt them to propel highway vehicles. The first Americans to do so successfully were Charles and Frank Duryea.

The Duryea brothers were something of opposites. Charles, eight years the elder, was a fast-paced individual with big ideas but a lack of persistence in fulfilling them. Frank, on the other hand, was a quiet, unassuming person with a stubborn work-streak that refused to permit him to leave a project until he had it bridled, saddled, and locked in a corral. Whereas Charles was boisterous and self-promoting, Frank was content to work in shy solitude.

In 1886, when Charles was twenty-five years old, he saw a gas engine that had been intended to fit onto a buggy. But the engine was so large and heavy that there was no chance for it to do anything more than hulk inertly over the carriage wheels. Nevertheless, the idea possessed Charles, and after reading a book by an Englishman five years later giving the outline of a smaller engine, Charles determined to construct such an engine to drive a carriage. To aid him in this enterprise, he brought in brother Frank, then working as a toolmaker for a manufacturing firm in Massachusetts.

In January 1892, Charles began pounding the streets of Springfield, Massachusetts to find a shop in which he and Frank could construct their exciting new vehicle. He would have preferred a first-floor workshop, but none seemed to be available at the price he could pay. So, after two months of searching, he had to settle for a large second-floor room above the Russell Manufacturing Company.

Right from the beginning, Charles's bright hopes were clouded by the disquieting fact that he had absolutely no money to buy the parts with which to make his car. To remedy this, he offered Erwin Markham 10 percent of the future profits in return for an investment of one thousand dollars. When Charles brought Markham diagrams of his projected auto, Markham looked them over carefully. But the poor fellow could learn very little, for nowhere in America had such an unusual bit of engineering been attempted. Had Markham refused to invest, it is unlikely that Charles, for all his enthusiastic talk and glittering promises, could have interested another. Markham agreed, however, and the venture was underway.

Charles immediately purchased a secondhand buggy—a rather dilapidated thing worth a bare $70. This done, he loaded his buggy into the Russell elevator and deposited it in the second-floor workshop. Next Charles brought in Frank at $17.90 per week. This was a rather odd sum which could just as easily have been rounded off to $18. But dimes were counting now, for it was easy for Charles to guestimate that with the cost of parts added to Frank's wage, Markham's $1,000 would run out within three-fourths of a year. The question was, Would this give them enough time to put together a salable car?

Work on the auto began April 4, 1892, when the brothers started cutting the buggy body away from the wheels and axles. After they put the body in a corner, they carried the rear axle to a blacksmith where they had a groove forged in the center into which their engine could be placed. For this work, Charles peeled out $7.45 to the blacksmith.

Now other expenses started coming. There was $2.40 to be paid for a flywheel and $5.67 for a cylinder casting. A few days later, when the foundry had finished the casting, Charles had to pay $6.94 to have a four-inch-wide piston slot bored in it. Soon other items began eating into the Duryea treasure: $.30 for a gas line, $1.00 for an exhaust tube, $.75 for axle clips, $4.00 for five gallons of cylinder oil.

The Duryeas strove to keep everything as cheap and uncomplicated as possible. For example, the engine was "extremely simple," Frank recalled. "It resembled a cast-iron pipe . . . with a flange at one end to which the cylinder head was to be bolted."

In order to cut costs, they scrounged around machine shops in Springfield and surrounding towns for the necessary assortment of castoffs, rather than having parts made specifically to fit their needs. Once Charles even traveled as far as

Hartford, Connecticut, where he ended up rummaging through a hot attic junk heap in the Pope Bicycle factory before finding some gears that could be worked into the auto plan. The brothers also made many parts themselves, taking advantage of a summer lull in the Russell Company's business to use one of their grinding lathes.

As the Duryeas worked together during the summer of 1892, the operation took on a festive air. They shared ice-cream cones during the hot afternoons and a sense of companionship developed that was later to sour in a quarter-century feud over who actually invented America's first successful gasoline car.

Despite the excitement, the work went very slowly—far more so than Charles had expected. There was so much endless fitting and grinding and discarding of parts that didn't work. There were, for example, the intake and exhaust valves which had to be fitted into openings drilled in the cylinder head. Although the intake valve opened automatically with the downward suction of the piston (thereby permitting gasoline to flow into the cylinder), a special device had to be made to permit the exhaust valve to be pushed open by the upward motion of the piston.

It wasn't only the intricacies of the engine that took much of their time and money. They had to strengthen the carriage frame with iron framework pieces to support the weight of the engine. Then, too, they had to make a drive belt that would convey the engine power to the rear wheels. There also had to be a clutch to disengage the belt from the engine so that it could be started without the sort of jerky violence that would send Hiram Maxim bouncing into the air.

As they worked, more problems assaulted them. There was the question of an ignition system to get the gas to explode once it was in the cylinder and so drive the piston. There was the problem of a carburetor to maintain a proper mixture of gas and air, since too much of one or the other would result in no ignition.

As for the transmission, should the gears be of rawhide, which was light but relatively weak, or iron, which was heavy and expensive? Would a drive belt of rubber be able to turn the axle drum? Or should the belt be of leather? Or maybe a metal chain would do a better job.

Possibly the most difficult of their many problems did not even concern the auto directly. This was the nagging worry about money to finance their work. Day after day the dollars flowed out. Yet just when they thought they were over one roadblock, another popped up demanding more expenses. What would happen if they ran out of money before they had a model that could be put into sales production?

After laboring all spring and summer, Charles had had enough. By September 1892, he was so discouraged about ever getting a workable car that he decided to dump the frustrating matter in Frank's lap. He entered into the hopefully more profitable bicycle manufacturing field with a company in Peoria. But Charles kept an interest in the enterprise and before he took the train to Illinois, he decided at least to try to start the little engine that had caused him and his brother so much work and worry.

Charles and Frank placed the engine on a board laid between a pair of sawhorses. The engine was ludicrously primitive. It still had no proper carburetor. Instead the Duryeas shot a spray of gas into the engine's intake valve by means of a perfume atomizer they had purchased at a local drugstore. Nor did the engine have batteries or spark plugs to explode the gas. To accomplish this, the Duryeas simply stuck a small copper tube into the cylinder head and heated it by means of a tippy alcohol burner to a point hot enough to burn the gas.

Oblivious of their difficulties, the Duryeas lit the burner and placed it under the ignition tube. Then one squeezed out a gas-air mixture from the atomizer while the other attempted to start the engine by gripping the rim of the flywheel and turning it violently.

They watched anxiously as the flywheel forced the piston up and down. The intake cycle drew gas into the cylinder with a soft sucking sound. The ignition tube grew hotter and hotter. Round and round Charles, then Frank, wrenched the flywheel. Soon their arms ached and their breath came in wheezes.

But it was useless. In exhaustion, they were forced to admit that the motor would not kick over.

Charles then went off to Illinois in disgust. Frank was left alone with the grease, the gears, and a virtually empty cashbox.

The lark days were over. Now the drudgery began. Autumn, 1892, came and evening chills made Frank's fingers numb. He had not even the most elementary handbook to tell him of all the blind alleys he was losing himself in. He worked far into the night. He skimped on food. He didn't sleep much. But he wouldn't give up. His stubborn nature would not permit that.

Yet he could not combat his own frail body. In October he began suffering throbbing headaches. At last, he had to admit that he was ill. Staggering into a hospital, he was informed that he had typhoid fever.

For an entire month Frank writhed on a hospital bed. When he was released on November 5, his landlord helped the weakened youth celebrate the event with the news that he no longer wished to have Frank as a tenant—he feared Frank might be a typhoid carrier. Fortunately, Frank found lodging with friends. Nevertheless, it wasn't until January 1893, that Frank was strong enough to resume his work.

During the next month and a half Frank made many improvements—including a carburetor to replace the ineffective perfume atomizer—and at last the long-awaited moment came when, with a cough and a wheeze, the motor roared into life! The walls shook with the noise and the workers in the Russell plant below worried that the building might collapse on them.

With the engine now functioning, Frank's next goal was to hook it up to the buggy. This he did by hoisting the engine into the metal framework which he and Charles had made when they were optimistic so long ago. Then Frank connected the flywheel to the buggy axle by means of a narrow rubber belt 1 ½ inches wide.

When the time came to see if the motor could actually get the buggy to move, John Russell, owner of the building, came up to the second floor to be sure that Frank did not wreck the shop with his car. As Russell watched critically, Frank lit his burner. When the ignition tube was hot, Frank straddled the engine, grasped the flywheel with both hands, and rotated it as rapidly as possible.

With an echoing series of explosions, the single piston caught. Thrilled, Frank turned, reached forward, and gingerly pushed a lever to engage the rubber drive-belt with a drum around the rear axle. Here, as Frank remembered it many years later, was what happened:

> Shifting the belt into action, the vehicle started. Having started it, I had no doubt that I could stop it. But the belt would not return to neutral. Fearful now that the chassis would strike the wall and be damaged, I let go of the shift

lever and, grasping the rear axle, was dragged a few feet in an attempt to prevent the machine from striking the wall.

Across the shop Frank and America's first car went: Frank tugging at the rear axle as his heels left black marks on the wood flooring. As Frank bumped against the wall, he glanced with embarrassment at John Russell. "Mr. Russell seemed to regard this performance as a huge joke," Frank recalled. "I have a distinct memory of his laughing heartily, and I know that he told many people about it during the following years, for the tale came back to me in several different forms."

The fact that America's automobile age opened with a head-on collision did not deter Frank Duryea. The car had moved under its own power, and that pleased him.

This road test—if it might be called that—took place early in February 1893. Duryea now labored diligently to make his little vehicle worthy of a run on an actual road. One of his improvements during this time was the addition of a cooling system. This "system" consisted of a pair of roughly hammered-out copper jackets. Frank clamped these jackets around the cylinder, leaving an opening at the top into which he poured water to cool the engine. When the heated water began steaming out, Frank would replenish it from a bucket that he carried in the car.

Yet, for all his labor, Frank realized that the engine was a jerry-built affair that could never compete with the most mangy nag. Who would want to buy an auto when one's arms would ache from the effort of turning the flywheel to start it? When one's ears would ring for hours from the thunderous clangor of exploding gas driving a screeching piston? When one's back would be simmered from steam hissing out of the open water jacket? When one's mind would always be fretting about the danger of a fire from the tippy alcohol ignition lamp? Writing disdainfully about the engine, Frank admitted, "It needed, before it would be ready for the street: a starting device, a new piston and connecting rod, a new and heavier flywheel . . . a muffler with suitable piping, and an electric ignitor, as I regarded the lamp-heated ignition tube as unreliable if taken out in the wind."

What actually should be done, Frank concluded regretfully, was to throw the whole motor out and start anew. But he was now nearly out of funds, having spent most of Markham's investment on this worthless motor. He knew he had no alternative but to hit the unsuspecting man for more money.

Around the first of March 1893, Frank told Markham that a year's work and the expenditure of one thousand dollars had resulted in an engine that belonged on a junk heap. But the knowledge gained was invaluable, Frank insisted. Just a little more money to make a new engine based on his experience, and they should have something worth producing commercially.

After what we may presume was a gulp of dismay and a sigh of misgiving, Markham agreed to drop more money into what he must have thought was beginning to become a bottomless pit.

Frank began working on his new engine. Throughout the spring and summer he fashioned his improvements. Soon he had a properly constructed water jacket, complete with piping extending to a small two-gallon water tank under the buggy seat and a pump to insure water circulation. He had, at the same time, been perfecting a muffler that tended to quiet the infernal motor din. In addition, he replaced the ridiculous alcohol burner with a battery of six wet cells. Indeed, the car was coming along so well that he and Markham even splashed a coat of paint on the aged buggy panels.

It was now mid-September 1893, and the buggy was at last ready for its first run on the open road!

> We stood the vehicle up on end, resting on its rear wheels, to take it down the elevator, and it was left in the area between the Russell and Stacy buildings until after dark, when Mr. Markham's son-in-law, Mr. Bemis, brought a harnessed horse and we pulled it out to his barn on Spruce Street.

It was a humiliating way for the first car to emerge before the world—rear end down an elevator, then drawn by horse through the night ("so no one will see us," Frank admitted) to a manure barn on the outskirts of town. But Duryea and Markham feared their creation just might snort itself apart when it encountered a hill, and they had no wish to brave the giggles and guffaws of the young and old townsfolk who would love to savor a joke at their expense.

At nine the next morning, September 20, Duryea opened the barn doors and pushed the buggy into the sunshine. With him were three companions, including a reporter for the local newspaper. The atmosphere was electric as the young inventor climbed into his seat. He adjusted the transmission and throttle from levers on the steering tiller, which was an adapted bicycle handle. Then he signaled and his companions began pushing.

Slowly the carriage moved forward. Gradually the pushers were able to increase its speed. Soon the men were almost running. Then Duryea prepared to put the car in gear. How many times he had rehearsed this moment in his mind!

The time came. Duryea joggled the proper lever. With staccato explosions, the motor took hold. The vehicle leapt out of the pushers' grasp. The men stopped, panting, as Duryea drove onward in a cloud of exhaust fumes. They looked at one another and grinned. A carriage moving without a horse! What a silly, thrilling sight!

Frank Duryea was elated. He felt the sharp September breeze in his face and the chunky road rocking the floorboard. He saw the trees jolt by. He turned the steering lever and the carriage responded more quickly than a horse. The motor roared behind him like a trained servant ready to do his bidding.

In his exuberance, Duryea nosed the carriage toward a six-inch earth curbing—a minor obstruction but a test of sorts for the car. Up the front end went—up and stopped! The engine whirred angrily. Duryea adjusted this, then that. The men who had been left behind came running up. Duryea did all he could, but the thin rubber belt that connected the engine with the rear axle refused to take the load. With great disappointment, Duryea had to admit that a horseless carriage which could not ascend a six-inch grade was not yet ready for the public.

Nevertheless, Frank was not discouraged. Two days later he sent an excited letter off to Charles. The transmission problem, he said, "does not wet me down at all." Continuing, he wrote, "if you have anything good in the line of positive gearing Chas., send it on—as I want to be full of ideas."

Frank evidently drew a blank with Charles in the matter of new ideas, but he kept working, and by November 9 was ready to give the car a second road test. The purpose was to determine if the substitution of a leather transmission belt for the rubber one would prove more satisfactory. The test was disappointing, for it showed that the leather belt tended to wear smooth when turning the axle drum. Although the belt firmed up when Duryea stopped and dumped water on it, he realized that that was hardly an efficient manner of driving.

Frank hauled the car back to his shop. He worked on it ten more days, then confidently prepared to give it a third road test. He offered the driving honors to Markham. But Erwin politely declined. It wasn't that he minded the jostling of the iron-rimmed wheels over the chuckholes. He could even stand the engine's shaking and the gears' irritating grinding. His main concern was that Frank had not bothered putting brakes on the car! Frank's assurance that the transmission would be a sufficient drag on downhill grades was not enough to induce his cautious partner into the buggy seat. Therefore, Frank let Will Bemis, Markham's son-in-law, have the honors.

The engine was started, Will let out the clutch, and the strange machine chugged jerkily down the street.

A newspaper reporter was again on the scene and he left a graphic description of this epic jaunt—Duryea's first real success:

> Residents in the vicinity of Florence Street flocked to the windows yesterday afternoon astonished to see gliding by in the roadway a common top carriage with no shafts and no horse attached. The vehicle is operated by gasoline and is the invention of Erwin Markham and J. F. Duryea. . . . The vehicle, which was operated by Mr. Bemis, started from the corner of Hancock Avenue and Spruce Street and went up the avenue . . . working finely. But when about halfway down the latter street it stopped short, refusing to move. Investigation showed that the bearing [or more probably the pesky drive-belt] had been worn smooth by the friction. A little water sprinkled upon it put it in running condition again.

Although this newspaper article, as well as a prior one, painted lyrical pictures of the "ingenious wagon" that was "running along the streets or climbing country hills without visible means of propulsion," neither Markham, who had financed it, nor Bemis, who had driven it, were nearly that optimistic. Bemis had actually told Duryea that "the thing is absolutely useless;" and Markham was still distressed that he had donated so much of his money to a twenty-five-year-old wastrel who had taken two and a half years to piece together a contraption that could not travel over a few city blocks without wearing down one or more parts.

It was a distressing time for Duryea. He now realized that "Charles's friction transmission" [as he disdainfully referred to the leather belt in later years] could never drive the car successfully over any distance. What was required was a system of transmission gears. But to make the improvements, Frank needed more money. He pleaded with Markham and showed him diagrams of his plans. Markham remained skeptical. Would the young man ever complete the car? Or would he be sponging up Markham's funds until he was dry as a desert mesa?

Finally, in desperation, Frank voluntered to work without a salary until the car was perfected. The offer of free labor apparently tipped the scales. With great reluctance Markham made one last donation, bringing his total to around three thousand dollars.

Frank worked furiously during November and December, hoping to complete his car before his slender savings ran out. David Nesbitt, his landlord, had to chase Frank to bed night after night at 2 A.M.; otherwise he would have sat up rearranging blueprints until dawn. Yet the perfect car did not materialize and Frank's funds grew more scant.

"The outlook was anything but bright," Frank wrote. By January 1894, "I had been without income for two months, borrowing to live. Charles had, from time to time, borrowed from me, and now owed me $800, but was not at this critical period able to return any of it." On January 18, partially to quiet his many creditors as well as to show Markham he was getting something for his money, Frank decided to bring his rebuilt car down from the second floor shop for a fourth road test.

Frank cranked the engine and it popped into life. Accompanied by a friend, whom Frank had taken to push the vehicle if it failed him, Frank drove down Taylor Street toward Markham's house. There were tense moments as the car groaned up the Worthington Street hill. But it chugged over it without the dismal sound of spinning transmission. Although a little while later a part dropped out of the engine, it did not seem to cause any particular difficulty. Thereafter, Frank's only concern was the hissing sound from the water jacket. He arrived at Markham's in a cloud of steam—a sight that failed to instill much confidence in his investor. Markham, justly skeptical of the smoking contraption, again refused a ride. Thereupon, Duryea and his friend rumbled off at the frightful speed of 10 mph. After covering about six miles and rousing all the dogs in town, Frank brought the car back to the Russell building. The test had been a complete triumph.

Yet Frank realized that even now he did not have a commercially competitive car. Before he dared suggest to Markham and brother Charles that they try to produce for the market, he would have to make many more improvements. For one, the iron-rimmed tires should be replaced by rubber ones. For another, the engine should have a second cylinder to give it more hill-climbing power. In addition, the present transmission gears of iron and rawhide should be converted to all-metal. Thus, even though the trial run in January was a success, Frank felt that he must make another entirely new engine that would incorporate all the improvements which nearly two years of experiments had shown were necessary.

But to make the third engine would require more capital. Where could he get it? Markham was dry and there were few, if any men, in Springfield who would care to put funds into such an outlandish enterprise as a carriage run by gears and gasoline. Again, as so often before, failure loomed ahead.

During February and March, Frank desperately worked out a detailed series of drawings which he hoped would attract potential investors. These were bad times for him, what with his rent and grocery bills unpaid. Yet his luck held, for somehow he soft-soaped one H. W. Clapp into backing him. Clapp agreed to furnish the funds to build the new engine and to try to organize a company which would begin manufacturing autos as soon as Duryea had completed and tested his model car.

While Frank labored on his car during 1894, other inventors around the country were beginning to putter and pound on engines to run horseless carriages. We have seen that by the end of the year Hiram Maxim would have a certain bouncy success with his motorcycle. This would lead him to the Pope Bicycle Company and the production of four-wheeled motorized vehicles. Ransom Olds, who had already run a steam-powered car, was tinkering with a gas engine. And an intense former farmer named Henry Ford had already constructed a tiny engine consisting of a one-inch-wide cylinder made of a gas pipe and a crude carburetor formed by his wife's splashing gasoline into the intake valve from a metal cup. Altogether, an estimated three hundred young, enthusiastic Americans were trying to construct America's first successful gasoline auto.

Frank Duryea did not know how many persons were progressing along the same lines as he, but he was aware that he must hurry if he would gain the competitive advantage. By mid-April 1895, he was ready to test drive his new car. The test was a roaring success, as he reported to his brother in a letter of April 25. He told Charles that the car could actually ascend hilly streets at up to seven miles an hour; and that it could overtake on the straightaway any horse cart it met. After another week's testing, Frank told his brother that "the wagon continues to run well. No trouble to keep it in order at all now. It is a surprise to all. Pleases all that see it."

But it was one thing to turn out an individual car and quite another to produce large numbers for public sales. For this it was vital to attract men to put funds into the company that Mr. Clapp was trying to form. On the basis of the car's performance around Springfield, Clapp had managed to interest a few potential investors. However, none of these persons knew enough about these newfangled auto-things to acertain whether or not it would be a good investment. What they needed was a really thorough auto inspection by an expert in the field. And so they called in Mr. Slater, a hard-nosed steam engine specialist from Connecticut. If he gave his approval, a production company would be formed. If he indicated thumbs down, there would be little likelihood that Duryea would ever produce commercially.

Slater arrived in July 1895. Accompanied by the possible investors, he gave the car a thorough scrutiny. After some time, Slater said he'd like to take a demonstration ride. Frank had a route around Springfield in mind. But Slater demanded to be driven to Westfield—a rugged round-trip excursion of eighteen miles!

Frank dared make no objection. As Slater perched himself in the low-backed seat, Frank cranked up the engine. The group wished them luck and Frank put the car into gear. The little buggy bounded forward on the journey that would decide its future.

The way led west across the Connecticut River. As the buggy wheels jolted over the bridge planking, Frank prayed nothing would be thrown loose. To his relief, all went well and they bounced down the bridge to the point where the main highway turned south toward Hartford. The Hartford road was broad and relatively well maintained, for it had been a thoroughfare from long before the days when John Adams had taken a carriage over it to the Continental Congress meeting in Philadelphia. But the route Slater had chosen was not John Adams's road. Slater pointed west down a sandy farmers' path toward the hamlet of Westfield. Frank gunned the engine and hit off into the semiwilderness.

The way paralleled the Westfield River. It led over steep hills where the engine groaned in lowest gear. There were tight curves and perilous downgrades. Perhaps the worst obstacle of all was the sand which grated against the exposed gears and sometimes caused the tires to spin without traction. By the time the car had managed to reach Westfield, both passengers knew they had been through an ordeal. Now all that remained was the nine mile return drive!

In many ways the return was worse than the outward trip. Certainly the tension in Frank's mind increased as the outcome of the trip drew nearer. He must have turned over and over all the things that could go wrong: a buggy spring could break, dust could clog the carburetor, a stray stone could crack the casing of one of the glass battery jars.

Scores of incidents could happen. And there was not a single shop outside of Springfield where capable repairs could be made.

Hills and sand; then more hills and more sandy car-traps. It seemed to Frank that the grueling nine miles would never be over. And all the while Slater remained erect as a school-teacher on his seat. Periodically he would tilt his head to hear the motor's stress or peer over the car's edge to watch the wheels slither through the sand.

At last, Frank spotted the Connecticut River bridge. Up the embankment he went, then over the rattling planks, and finally down into Springfield. A feeling of joy welled up within him. He had done it! Eighteen miles without the car's falling apart! He beamed at Slater. The expert nodded his approval. Frank's beloved creation was a success!

Upon Slater's glowing report, four men immediately purchased stock and joined Frank and Charles in forming the Duryea Motor Wagon Company. After returning fidgety Erwin Markham's investment to him (along with a two-thousand-dollar profit), the company began the business of making cars. Frank provided the blueprints for an improved model, which he called his Buggyaut. Then a little factory was obtained, a labor force recruited, and by the end of the following year Duryea had turned out thirteen identical cars. Mass production had come to automobile manufacturing.

America was at the threshhold of a new age.

3

The Great Chicago Race

Herman Kohlsaat, publisher of the Chicago *Times-Herald*, had a brilliant idea to increase circulation. Why not stage a race between those horseless-carriage things that were beginning to pop up in various parts of the country! Just the last Fourth of July in Kokomo, Indiana—not too far from Chicago—a car invented by Elwood Haynes had been the hit of the parade. In Chicago itself, an electric car built by William Morrison of Des Moines had created such public interest that it couldn't be driven downtown without a ring of policemen to clear gawkers from its path.

Kohlsaat knew a *Times-Herald* race was one heck of an idea. Thus, when he announced that he would award five thousand dollars in prizes, he was not surprised that the story made front pages in newspapers across the country. He was surprised, however, when he received not the five or ten entry telegrams that he expected, but over sixty. Within weeks, the total entries reached nearly a hundred!

Kohlsaat could hardly believe there were so many persons working on horseless carriages. He pictured one hundred vehicles roaring down the race-route from Chicago to Milwaukee and back—a total of two hundred miles. What an event it would be! It would even put the famed Paris to Belfort competition of 1894 to shame. Although this had been the world's first large race (twenty-five cars had started and fifteen finished), the Chicago event would be the first in this hemisphere.

Kohlsaat had planned to stage the great race on the Fourth of July, 1895. But when a majority of the entrants said they could not get their machines ready by that time, he reluctantly postponed the race until November 2, probably the last date before Indian Summer gave way to winter.

Frank and Charles Duryea eagerly planned for the race. Frank, shy and quiet, spent endless hours perfecting his little machine. He worked on it until his hands had unsightly calluses, until his muscles ached, until he grew thin and pale. He spoke and thought of nothing except his horseless carriage. Charles, bold and blustery, wanted to take credit for the Buggyaut. But to him it was merely a means toward wealth. To Frank, it was a personal creation, a thing with a soul.

The Chicago contest was extremely important for the Duryeas. They had just formed a company to manufacture their Buggyaut and a victory at Chicago was vital to their plans. Should they lose to one of the Benz cars, the German firm which produced them would have a clear shot at the American market. It could be that almost the entire United States would become an economic satellite of European car makers, who were advanced over the Americans in many technical matters.

The Duryeas were not the only American inventors hard

at work preparing models for the big race. Elwood Haynes, of Kokomo fame, had a nice horseless carriage that convinced those who saw it he would win the race. Hiram Maxim had a horseless carriage that ran when it was in the mood. Indeed, in dozens of barns and horse stables across the nation hammers pounded and engines sputtered. Men talked of spark plugs, of carburetors, of gears and clutches and transmissions. October came. The hammering became more frantic; the engine failures more frustrating.

Then it was November 2—the day of the race. A crowd gathered in the warm sunshine in Jackson Park. Ladies sported colorful parasols and gentlemen wore shiny derbies. There was excitement in their conversation, for they were about to see the first auto race ever held in the United States.

But publisher Kohlsaat held up his hands for an announcement. He was sorry, he said, but the race would have to be postponed until Thanksgiving, November 28. The reason was that the only cars able to chug to the starting gate were a Benz driven by Oscar Mueller and the Buggyaut with Frank Duryea at the wheel.

As murmurs of discontent rose, Kohlsaat continued. He was pleased to say that Duryea and Mueller had agreed to a private exhibition between the American and German machines. The first car to make it up and back to Waukegan—ninety miles—would receive a purse of five hundred dollars.

The crowd roared its approval. Duryea and Mueller warmed up their engines.

At a signal from the starting judge, they were off!

Frank and Charles Duryea leaped ahead. Soon their lead was lengthened as Mueller had to repair a tire. But then the Duryeas' drive-chain snapped. As they worked to fix it, Mueller passed them, a great smile on his face.

Once their chain was functioning, the Duryeas were back

in the race. As they neared Chicago's northern border, the American car inched past the Benz. Slowly, the Buggyaut continued to pull away.

Suddenly, in front of them, a horse wagon started across the street. The Duryeas let loose with a blast from their foghorn, but the wagon kept moving. At the last minute Frank was forced to swerve off the road to miss the wagon. The Buggyaut smashed into a ditch and was unable to continue.

Mueller made the round trip, averaging 10 mph. He collected the prize money and the laurels of victory.

The Duryeas vowed that they would not lose to a Benz when the main race was held on the twenty-eighth.

As the twenty-eighth approached, it appeared that eleven inventors had their contraptions adjusted so that they could at least reach the starting line in Jackson Park. If the weather was good and the roads not muddy, most of these drivers figured they could hold their autos together long enough to rumble over the course.

But, during the afternoon of the twenty-seventh, a bitter November storm began slicing through the Windy City. By nightfall heavy snow was falling. When the drivers woke on Thanksgiving morning, they realized there was little to give thanks for about this day. A vile mixture of snow and slush nearly half a foot deep had splattered itself over the route to Milwaukee.

Herman Kohlsaat and the *Times-Herald* would not postpone the race yet another time—it had already fizzled twice. The publisher announced that the race would begin at 9 A.M. Let him who could participate do so. As a concession to Mother Nature, however, the route would be diminished from the two hundred miles to and from Milwaukee, to fifty-two miles round trip to Evanston.

With that, there was a great scurrying among contestants to purchase rope to tie around their car wheels, thereby converting them into the world's first snow tires.

Frank Duryea had risen before dawn. The snow crackled beneath his feet as he walked to the Buggyaut. He carefully checked it over for the last time. The motor started, but how weak it sounded in the early morning quiet! Was it possible that his frail, two-cylinder machine could push the carriage through this evil obstruction of slush for fifty-two miles?

Frank realized he could do nothing more than hope. He steered his car out into the street and headed toward Jackson Park. It was slippery going, he noted. Probably a worse day for racing could not have been chosen.

When Duryea got to Jackson Park, he found two vehicles there ahead of him. One was called an Electrobat. It fascinated the few women spectators with its smooth, quiet, electric ride—so superior to the smelly, smoke-belching gas cars. Nearby was one of the feared Benzes, this sponsored by Macy's Department Store of New York, which might act as a distributor for the German firm as it tried to take over the American market. Jerry O'Conner, an expert driver, was at the Macy-Benz wheel.

Soon Duryea and the others were joined by a Sturges Electric car and then by the Benz which had won against all European competition.

As the starting time approached, race officials sent inquiries about the other cars. Word came back that most of the other cars, for various reasons, could not get started. This left absent only the Benz driven by Oscar Mueller, the Duryeas' arch-rival. It was reported that Mueller would soon be there: he had been delayed by trouble with his drive-belt.

Kohlsaat was determined that his race should not be postponed again, not even for a matter of minutes. Mueller would just have to start late and take the penalty. The contestants were told to get ready.

There was silence as Judge C. F. Kimball looked at his watch. It read 8:55. He cupped his hands. "Go!" he shouted.

The cars were to start on a staggered basis. Each driver was to be accompanied by a referee to be certain he took no shortcuts to victory. Frank Duryea and referee Arthur White were the first to leave. At Kimball's word, they leaped into the Buggyaut. Frank's heart was thumping, for the future of his car, as well as perhaps the future of America's infant auto industry, rode on how well he drove against the German competition. He knew he would be pushed all the way by the three Benzes waiting to take the crown to Europe.

Duryea drove rapidly through the sunlit snow. Spectators snapped photos of him with their Kodaks, for their friends in other cities would certainly not believe in such a fanciful invention as a carriage run without a horse unless they could see pictures with their own eyes.

One minute after Duryea shot off, the Paris-Champion Benz got the go-ahead. Quickly after it came the Macy-Benz driven by hotshot Jerry O'Conner. At 9:01 the Sturges Electric whirred off in silent majesty. Sixty seconds later the Electrobat entered the race, with an excited Hiram Maxim aboard as contest referee. Oscar Mueller and his Benz still had not reached the starting point.

The cars hurried west until they reached Michigan Boulevard. There they turned north toward Evanston. It was near

Frank Duryea in his prize-winning car, 1895. (CHICAGO HISTORICAL SOCIETY)

this point that the first of the cars was forced to withdraw. The Paris champion could win a French race, but in Chicago it failed to surmount a pile of snow! With the Benz's transmission slipping badly, the driver gave up in despair.

Michigan Avenue was a straightaway where throttles could be opened wide. Cheering crowds waved as the Buggyaut, followed by the Macy-Benz chugged past. Soon the racers reached Chicago's fashionable residential area. High society did not care to stand with the commoners in the cold, but "at the windows of the wealthy and the notable [ran the *Times-Herald* racing edition] there were clusters of faces—children, the matrons, the fathers, and the babies."

The total number of persons jamming Michigan Avenue was estimated to be upwards of ten thousand. Nearly every policeman in town was on foot, bike, or horseback to control the spectators. Everyone was in a holiday mood, though, and there were no unruly incidents at this time.

The two electric cars were trailing Duryea and O'Conner. Hiram Maxim squirmed uncomfortably aboard one of them, surely wishing he had been able to iron the many bugs out of his gas car and enter the race. The batteries were no match for the thick slush which resisted the car's progress and after a few miles both electric car drivers were forced to admit that their quiet, graceful buggies were outclassed by the growling, bucking gasoline machines. This left just Frank Duryea and Jerry O'Conner in the race.

About this time, however, Oscar Mueller and his Benz reached the starting line. With a wave to the starter, he roared off in pursuit. Since he was more than an hour late, he had a tough task ahead. Yet all was not lost. For the leaders were having problems that might well throw the race to Mueller.

O'Conner had the first difficulty. Daredevil that he was, he decided to ride the streetcar rails in preference to the chopped-up pavement. That was fine until a streetcar ahead of him came to a sudden stop. O'Conner was unable to brake on the slippery rails. With a crunch, he plunged into the rear of the streetcar. No one was hurt, for O'Conner's speed had been hardly faster than that of a strolling pedestrian. With the aid of spectators, the Benz was lifted off the tracks. Then O'Conner sputtered on.

Meanwhile Frank Duryea was also having trouble. His steering lever broke just before he reached the Rush Street bridge. Leaving his machine in the street, Duryea rushed to a nearby blacksmith shop, where a new steering arm was forged. It took nearly an hour before Duryea was again in the race! While he was fussing helplessly, O'Conner took the lead.

At 10:30, O'Conner rattled through Lincoln Park. Here he came upon rooters assembling for the Thanksgiving Day football game between the universities of Michigan and Chicago. The crowd waved its pennants of maize and blue or maroon and white enthusiastically. Not even the whinny of frightened horses could detract from the amazing sight of a gasoline carriage actually running at the speed of six miles an hour!

Duryea reached Lincoln Park forty minutes behind O'Conner. Although he was plowing through the slush at eight miles an hour, only about half the football crowd remained to see this marvel of modern science. When Oscar Mueller puffed into the park a half hour later it was almost deserted. But he and his two riders had no time for hand-waving anyway; they were too busy sprinkling sand on the drive-belt to keep it from slipping.

The first relay station was at Sheridan Road and Grace Street. O'Conner popped in a little after 11:00. There was a large gathering of spectators, including some boys who had passed the time by snowballing carriages. While O'Conner took on oil, water, and a heap of ice to cool his engine, two policemen kept curious persons from overrunning the car. After a couple of minutes, the Macy-Benz was on its way.

Soon the Duryea car, in hot pursuit, approached. With

every mile it was gaining on the Benz. Duryea did not even stop at the relay station. Instead he passed through the crowd without slackening his blistering pace of 8 mph. Duryea's referee, Art White, yelled out as his car bowled northward along Sheridan Road, "How far ahead is the other fellow?" A policeman shouted back, "Twenty minutes." "We'll overhaul him pretty soon," was White's confident reply as the car disappeared in a flurry of slush and smoke.

The onlookers shook their heads. Twenty minutes was too long a lead. It couldn't be done. Duryea had lost to a Benz before and he would do so again. The Germans were just too good at mechanical things.

When Oscar Mueller reached the relay station shortly thereafter, the crowd's pessimism concerning Duryea was confirmed. With a Benz in front of him and another Benz gobbling up the miles behind, it seemed apparent that Duryea had little chance of winning.

Frank Duryea kept his accelerator open as far as he dared as he sped over the ice and slush that glazed the surface of Sheridan Road. On his left, the buildings and prairie lands of Chicago's farthest reaches fled behind him. On his right the blue waters of Lake Michigan, chopped and ruffled by the sharp November wind, splashed against snowy sands. Ahead he made out the sharp bend where Sheridan arched around the bleached tombstones of Calvary Cemetery. As he made the turn, he saw a weatherworn marker indicating the town limits of Evanston.

Skirting Calvary Cemetery, Duryea spotted O'Conner in the distance. He glanced at Art White. They both let out a whoop.

O'Conner saw Duryea gaining on him. He gunned his

Benz. But Duryea kept narrowing the gap. Evanstonians gathered about an industrial school at Sheridan and Main shouted for their favorite as the two cars passed. More spectators were clustered along Sheridan before the fine mansions of the wealthy lakeshore residents. Duryea kept pushing his Buggyaut. O'Conner, in desperation, did everything he could to keep the lead, but still Duryea kept eating up the distance between them. By the time the two racing cars reached Forest Avenue, Duryea was so close to the Benz that he could smell its exhaust. Then, while the people along the roadside yelled excitedly, Duryea inched up to the European car. The Benz had no fenders over a portion of the rear wheel and Duryea had no windshield to protect him from the slush that the Benz flung out. But what did a little slush in the face matter to Duryea? He was all smiles, for he was about to take the lead!

According to contest rules, when one car was about to pass another, the lead car had to pull to the side of the road. O'Conner did this, to the applause of the crowd. Then the two cars, almost bumper to bumper, turned west on Davis Street, Evanston's main thoroughfare, toward Chicago Avenue, where the trip south to Jackson Park would begin.

Evanston's biggest crowd was gathered around the Davis-Chicago corner—more people even than had watched the bicycle races earlier in the year, reported the impressed *Times-Herald*. The crowd's tension was high, for the storm had broken telephone communication with Chicago and none of those assembled knew how the race was going. It was only around 12:45 when cheers from Forest Avenue reached them that the Davis Street spectators realized the long-awaited moment was about to arrive.

The crowd screamed as Duryea, closely followed by

O'Conner, edged around the Davis-Chicago corner. Young boys dashed alongside the two cars, and men and women in carriages rode behind. For a while it became almost a parade.

As the two cars swung down Chicago Avenue, they picked up even more carriages and sleighs. One of these was a cutter in which the driver of the Paris-champion Benz rode with contest officials. This cutter was between Duryea and O'Conner as they crossed the railroad tracks near Evanston's southern border. But here the cutter's runners caught in a rail groove. With a great shudder, the cutter toppled on its side, throwing its passengers into O'Conner's path. As he jerked his steering gear to miss them, he smashed into the sleigh's side. It was his second collision of the race!

Once again spectators helped O'Conner get his vehicle back on the road. Then he resumed his pursuit of Duryea. But soon after reentering Chicago, O'Conner saw a horse buggy pull out of a cross street. Despite O'Conner's yells, the driver refused to heed his right-of-way. O'Conner tried to swerve out of the buggy's path, but his front wheel hit the hack's rear tire. It was his third collision of the race!

When O'Conner assessed the damage, he found four wheel spokes badly damaged and the steering gear bent and nearly useless. So many things had gone wrong that by this time he was taking the whole thing with a wry grin and shrug of the shoulders. O'Conner continued, riding the tracks of the Clark Street trolley, where the rail grooves did the steering for him. Reaching the second relay station at Clark and Devon, O'Conner spent an hour and twenty minutes on repairs. He also took on seven gallons of water and used a Niagara of naphtha to clean spattered crankcase oil from his engine. Not until 2:37 was O'Conner back on Duryea's trail.

The Mueller Benz was fifty-one minutes behind O'Conner, having had its share of trouble with a clutch bent by the rough roads.

Duryea was now supposedly far ahead. But when race officials in a sleigh a quarter mile behind him asked the people gathered along Ashland Avenue if they had seen the Buggyaut, they shook their heads. The confused officials drove farther on. Again they asked the spectators about Duryea. Again their responses confirmed that he had not passed along the race route. Where could he be?

While heads were being scratched on Ashland Avenue, Duryea and referee White were clomping down Clark Street merrily unaware that they had missed a hand-written arrow directing them down Ashland. After a while Duryea became concerned. Where were the crowds? Why did those persons who saw him react with such astonishment? One lady had even dropped her packages and run down a side street! Gradually he became aware that he was far off course. Anxiously turning west on Diversey, he planned to regain the race route as quickly as possible.

As he hurried west, his engine began to misfire. Soon the buggy was bucking like an unbroken mustang. Duryea curbed the beast, then ran down the street searching for a tinsmith shop where he could have a new sparking device made. At last he found such a shop. With relief he turned the door handle. It was locked! Frantically Duryea asked passersby where the owner's home was. After a few moments he learned the location and dashed to the tinsmith's bungalow. Pounding on the door, Duryea was dismayed to learn that the smithy was still in bed—although it was midafternoon! Duryea finally got the tinsmith to his shop. But then he had to wait while the smithy lighted his fire, bellowed it into heat, and slowly forged a new sparking device. It wasn't until 3:10 —after fifty-five agonizing minutes of waiting—that Duryea was back in the race.

By the time Duryea reached the assigned route, the day was growing dusky and turning colder. Knots of persons waiting to see the tardy cars had grown unruly. At Douglas Park, rowdies began what the *Times-Herald* politely called "snowball parties." Soon snowballs were flying with such ferocity that police decided to make some arrests. Then "the crowd turned loose on them with their white missiles [ran the *Times-Herald* account] and completely drove them for a time from the street. Two hundred small boys charged one officer, knocked his hat from his head, covered him with snow, and made him retreat. An attempt to call for the patrol wagon revealed the fact that not a telephone nor police alarm box in that district had been working since the storm."

Such frolicking evidently wore out the crowd, for by the time Duryea came through Douglas Park around 6 P.M., the only person to greet him was a *Times-Herald* reporter, dutifully standing in the dark stamping his feet and puffing on his hands.

Meanwhile Jerry O'Conner had been trying to maintain his pace. With his motor crying in agony, his steering gear unresponsive, and his wheels wobbly and out of line, O'Conner kept his machine going only from persistence and the consummation of a lifetime's Irish luck. Upon entering Douglas Park at 6:15, O'Conner's plucky assortment of bolts, belts, and buckboards refused to go on. The Benz sputtered to a halt and O'Conner got out his tools. Try as he might, it was to be a futile operation, for the contraption would never run again.

But what had happened to Oscar Mueller?

Mueller was being beset by the weather. With no wind-shield to give him protection from the icy wind nor any heating device to give him warmth, Mueller found racing on this wintery day to be almost beyond his endurance. He was further weakened by the lack of food, for his breakfast had been inadequate and he had had only a single small sand-wich for lunch. It was so bad riding in the exposed car that one of Mueller's observers, Charles Reid, had lost conscious-ness and been lifted into a passing sleigh. Mueller, shivering and blue-lipped, had continued the race, accompanied by contest official, Charlie King.

By the time Mueller passed O'Conner working futilely on his junk heap in the blackness of Douglas Park, Mueller was woozy from his empty stomach, the buffeting wind, and the bone-numbing cold. Turning east down the Garfield Boule-vard homestretch, Mueller slumped unconscious over the steering lever. Charlie King, the contest referee, shoved him to one side and took over himself.

But by now it was too late to overtake Frank Duryea. He had already sped down Garfield, where he and his referee had, in the words of the *Times-Herald*, given "vent to war-whoops, cheers, catcalls and other manifestations of joy over the victory they were winning." Despite the cold, everything was fun for Duryea and White now.

At the Halsted crossing they laughed as a handsome woman with a finely dressed, aristocratic escort jumped back in fright as the strange rig approached her out of the darkness. Shortly thereafter, a bunch of drugstore cowboys trotted alongside Duryea, laughing and shouting with excitement, until Duryea left them panting in the distance.

After a four-minute wait for a slow-moving railroad train, Duryea made the final lap to the finish line in Jackson Park. It was now 7:18 P.M., and there were only a few spectators braving the frigid darkness to welcome him. Yet their cheers echoed sharp and joyful in the November wind.

Frank Duryea climbed out of the mud-splattered Buggyaut. Then he steadied himself against the side as he accepted the victory handshakes. The quiet man beamed broadly. He had beaten Europe's finest autos while establishing a world's record of fifty-two miles through snow in only ten hours and twenty-three minutes. For the first time it seemed assured that America had a future in the automotive field. It was a great day for Duryea and for his country.

4

The Midnight Ride
of Hiram Maxim

Hiram Maxim returned from the great Chicago race flaming with enthusiasm for horseless carriages. Colonel Albert Pope, America's largest bicycle manufacturer, had already put young Hiram on his payroll and, after Chicago, directed him to devote his energies to the perfection of an electric vehicle. It was Pope's belief than an electric would attract wealthy, genteel buyers who might be repelled by a noisy gasoline car. "You can't get people to sit over an explosion," was the Colonel's favorite saying. Hiram, having ridden on a defunct electric at Chicago, found it difficult to share his boss's sunny feeling toward battery-driven cars. However, he could admit that they had their place—for short runs— on paved city streets, driven by persons who didn't have to get anywhere very quickly.

Hiram, as the Chief (and only) Auto Engineer of the Pope

Bicycle Works, built a snappy little electric buggy. As the leaves began to unfurl in the spring of 1896, Hiram began taking his silent oddity, called the Mark I, down the streets of Hartford, Connecticut. The trial runs were successful. Colonel Pope thereupon took the graceful little electric to his heart and ordered full-scale production. Within a few years the Pope Bicycle Company was selling two thousand motor vehicles yearly. Through Maxim's efforts Hartford became the electric car capital of the world. Pope was selling more cars than all other American manufacturers combined!

But Maxim was still not convinced that an electric car was the best bet in the long run. An electric could travel only about 12 mph and make only twenty-five miles before requiring a recharge. That was hardly the type of vehicle to replace good old Dobbin.

Hiram had plenty of reasons to maintain his interest in gas buggies. All he had to do was keep track of the Duryeas. In April 1896, Barnum and Bailey featured the Buggyaut in its circus parade, where it was an attraction shading the other freaks. Then, in November, the Duryeas entered a race held in England to celebrate the long-overdue repeal of the red-flag law. This race was between London and Brighton, about the same distance as the Chicago event a year earlier. But now there were more than forty cars—some of the best in Europe. Frank Duryea, in his little contraption, was given a nice spot in the rear. It took him fully half the race to dodge through the stalled cars that soon littered the road. Once he was through though, he opened his car up. Crossing the finish line, Duryea lolled around for an entire hour before the second car sputtered home.

Duryea's dramatic victory stunned many proud European

manufacturers. One wealthy British bicycle maker offered Frank a quarter-of-a-million dollars in cash for the distribution rights to his Buggyaut. But it was brother Charles, not Frank, who was in control of the company. Charles and his associates were back in the States. They did not respond with proper speed and the Englishman's interest turned to other fields. In such a manner did opportunity hammer at the Duryeas' door and find no one home. Thereafter, the brothers split in anger. Both would manufacture cars, but neither would achieve the success that had hovered within their grasp in 1896.

Meanwhile, in Hartford, Colonel Pope was still in love with his electric cars. Nonetheless, one day late in 1896 he called Maxim into his office and told his Chief Engineer to build a gasoline-powered delivery wagon. The Colonel felt that if the exhaust-coughing vehicle kept to the alleys and back ways it would probably be of some use, and at the same time not offend the elegant ladies and gentlemen taking the breeze in their spotless Mark I electrics.

Hiram threw himself into the project with his usual enthusiasm. Soon he came up with an elongated three-wheeled vehicle in the center of which was a large bin about five feet long and three feet high that could hold a merchant's goods. The rig was steered by a man on a bicycle saddle sitting in the rear. In order to start the gas engine, as well as help it ascend hills, Maxim included a pair of bicycle pedals connected by a chain to the rear wheels.

By February 1897, the Mark VII delivery truck was ready to run. As the weather was still too bad for a road test, Maxim could only guide his little vehicle around the abandoned top floor of the Hartford Typewriter Company. With the coming of March, however, he decided to run it out-doors. What did he care if the roadways were still only rivers of mud, for, as he put it, "I hungered day and night for the open road."

His first ventures were limited successes. As long as he kept to Hartford's rutted back streets, his little engine chugged along quite well. But each time that he turned onto the paved road by the City Hall (where crowds gathered to gawk at him) the pesky engine coughed and sputtered and gasped and groaned—and inevitably stopped entirely. Amid the smart-aleck catcalls of "Get a horse!" Hiram had to push the dead car down the street. Once he was beyond the snickers, the engine would hum into action once more. It happened day after day and was absolutely infuriating! It was almost as if the engine was alive and was mocking him.

At last Maxim discovered the cause. It was his carburetor —or, rather, lack of carburetor—that was causing the engine to stop. Maxim had found that air passing through the top of the gas tank just naturally became mixed with the proper amount of gas vapor to form an explosive mixture when it entered the cylinder. Since this was the case, why burden himself with a carburetor?

The problem was that Maxim assumed all roads were rutted and gouged and that the resulting swish-swish of the gas in the tank would provide sufficient agitation for a good gas-air mixture. But the unexpected block of smooth pavement around the City Hall calmed the gasoline. The result was a diminution of gas vapor causing the motor to die for lack of a proper fuel mixture.

The carburetor problem was just one of the many that Maxim—as well as all the other motor-tinkerers—were hav-ing at this time. Gradually Maxim met and solved most of his difficulties. Then came the thrilling day when he felt ready to take his machine into that distant, dangerous place called the country.

It was in the spring of 1897 that Maxim, and a happy-go-lucky friend named Eugene Lobdell decided to safari into the country. Once the country had been linked to civilization by well-maintained roads. But that was before the railroads had extended networks throughout the nation between 1850 and 1880. After that the travelers who had once demanded good highways took railroad trains to their destinations. The country was left to the farmers. Intercity highways gradually fell apart, as the only roads receiving maintenance were those short ones that led from the farms to the local railroad depots. Thus road conditions in the country were almost as primitive in 1897 as they had been when the pioneers first chopped their way into the wilderness three or four generations earlier.

Hi and Gene's first venture into the country was a fiasco. They intended to make their way from Hartford to Springfield, a heart-clutching trip of twenty-five miles. A hundred years earlier such a trip was routine, and John Adams had called the trip out of Hartford "the finest ride in America." But now Hiram could hardly even get out of town. At Hartford's limits he met a world that Adams had not known:

> We advanced about a hundred yards, wallowing and slithering sidewise in the dark [of course they left at dusk to escape the jests of local humorists], Lobdell pushing and pulling, and everything else jangling, clattering, and rattling as the poor little engine struggled under the heavy load [the load being only featherweight Maxim]. Happening to glance down, I saw the cylinder head of the engine glowing in the dark. It was red hot [—which would make Hiram place a water jacket around his next engine for cooling]. I

had never seen a gasoline engine running red hot before, and it appeared the better part of wisdom to pause a moment and look matters over. As things stood we would require about a month to reach Springfield!

They tried for a while to travel on the track of an electric trolley, but the mud between the wooden ties was so soft that each tie became a tooth-crunching bump. And so they turned back to Hartford, completely defeated. The distance traveled had been a quarter of a mile!

Two weeks later the two adventurers made another attempt to get out of Hartford. The road was drier now and the engine had new bearings. But Maxim found that a dry road was in some respects even worse than a wet one. In particular, there were the potholes made by farmers' wagons. These obstructions were too numerous to dodge. Eventually Hi and Gene found themselves banging down one hole after the other. Like a bucking bronco, the little delivery truck clambered along the road, the engine straining in agony.

Two miles out of Hartford, the country won. There was a loud crying sound from the engine and the car came to a sudden stop. Thus ended Maxim's second attempt to reach Springfield.

When May came, the persistent pair set out again. By now the potholes had been planed down into only mildly deep chuckholes by the iron-rimmed wheels of the farmers' wagons. Soon they passed the quarter-mile limit of their first attempt, and later the two-mile limit of their second. They let out a whoop and opened the motor up to a fantastic speed of 12 mph. The two men felt that they were fairly burning up the roadway—and they were if they compared their progress with the gait of a horse drawing a wagon. But horses rarely had to stop, whereas the motorists were forced

Top: a muddy road, 1905. Bottom: two Curved Dash Olds stuck in the mud.

to halt every fifteen minutes to pour a cup of heavy oil into the engine's leaking crankcase.

Hi and Gene found that there were many other obstructions to maintaining their breakneck speed. One was the horses they encountered, for every horse that saw this frightful contraption noise-maker went into an almost uncontrollable panic. Only by parking at the side of the road with their engine off could they expect a horse-drawn vehicle to pass by without incident. And it wasn't only horses who viewed the clattering delivery truck with distrust. Some humans were equally frightened by the mechanical monster, as Maxim found when he stopped at the roadside to permit a carriage to pass:

> Just as I pulled over, one of the men in the carriage, evidently having seen all he cared for, precipitately dismounted from the carriage. I immediately recognized him as one of my neighbors in Hartford. Evidently he had recognized me and was persuaded that something terrible was about to occur. Not satisfied with getting out of the carriage, he hurried to the side of the road, climbed the fence, and started on the dead run across the open field, apparently with the purpose of getting over the horizon as quickly as possible.

After a good laugh, Hi and Gene continued on their way. They rumbled through the village of Windsor Locks, "kicking up the biggest sensation in the little main street since the hotel burned." Past Windsor Locks the way was deserted. It was around midnight and their only illumination was from a small kerosene light joggling over the front wheel. The chuckholes were real dangers, now, for even with the vehicle going hardly faster than a man could walk, there was little chance to dodge the holes in the flickering, sputtering lantern light.

Nevertheless, the two of them were having the time of their lives. Chugging through the balmy darkness on a route that had never before heard the roar of a horseless carriage was an exhilarating adventure.

Suddenly they saw something ahead:

> In the flickering glow of the kerosene headlamp there appeared to be an enormous animal of some kind reared up on its hind legs, pawing the air with its forelegs and snorting. I could hear the snorts above the noise of our engine. The sight was one well calculated to freeze the blood in one's veins.

After a suspenseful moment, Maxim and Lobdell realized that the figure ahead was a wagon horse. Fearing that the terrified beast might damage the truck, they both leaped to the ground and dashed to get hold of the animal's bridle. But just as they reached the horse, he let loose with a kick that whanged the truck's front wheel apart. It was a distressful accident, but not totally unexpected, for they had been through similar experiences with other horses and had the proper tools and spare parts to resurrect the wheel.

It was the driver, not the horse, who caused them their main concern. He was literally in a state of shock.

> I grasped the situation at once. This junk-dealer, bringing a load of junk to Windsor Locks in the silent night, was blissfully ignorant of the existence of such a thing as a motorized vehicle. As he wended his way along the lonely country road, up from the distance came a strange and unearthly noise, the like of which he had never heard in all his life. This weird noise became a din. The din grew louder and signified that whatever was making the awful sound was approaching. A little flickering light appeared ahead, and as he strove to make out what could be making such a racket

he thought of everything he had ever seen on the road before. Could it be a mowing machine: a steam fire-engine? Before he could judge its distance in the dark the monstrous thing was upon him and about to run him and his horse down.

Maxim and Lobdell, in the mischievous spirit of youth, chided the petrified junkman for permitting such a wild animal as his horse to obstruct the roads. With that they sent the confused man on his way and a short while later were themselves back on the long haul to Springfield.

Now there were only the regular pauses to tighten up the bolts that were constantly jarring loose and to dump more oil into the crankcase. Chatting and chuckling, they found the time passed quickly. At last they saw the lights of Springfield across the Connecticut River. It was about three o'clock in the morning as they rattled over the same bridge that had creaked to Duryea's Buggyaut several years earlier. Then they turned down the dark streets, startling several sleepy policemen as they passed.

They headed for the Massasoit Hotel. There was a stable behind the hotel where they intended to house the Mark VII for the night. As they approached the stable, a bleary-eyed man ran out, a lantern held over his head. From the horrible engine roar, he thought that a locomotive had jumped the nearby track and was clawing down upon him!

Gene Lobdell jumped from the car and hurried over to the trembling watchman. Always a wiseacre, Gene brought his face up to the man's and asked excitedly, "Is this Philadelphia?"

Who knows what thoughts must have jumbled through the man's mind. What infernal machine was this that could overshoot Philadelphia by two hundred miles and the driver not know it!

"My God!" the watchman gasped. "This is Springfield, Massachusetts!"

Lobdell, not content to let the moment pass, called back in mock surprise to Hiram, "He says this is Springfield, Massachusetts!"

After a second of silence they both let out peals of laughter. The watchman grinned, then he joined them.

5

The Fantastic Little Curved Dash

A few months after Hiram Maxim's adventuresome midnight ride from Hartford, Ransom E. Olds decided to form a company to make horseless carriages. Although Olds was a modest and soft-spoken gentleman, those who knew him were impressed with his self-confidence and determination. Furthermore, he had sterling qualifications to enter the gasoline vehicle field. As a man of thirty-three, he had been associated with cars and machine shops for many years.

Ransom's father had been a blacksmith, and as a young boy Ransom had constantly been around buggies and other wheeled vehicles in the blacksmith shop. Then, when Ransom was sixteen, his father had established a machine repair shop in Lansing, Michigan. Ransom spent long hours in the shop after high school and even during his vacations, repairing the steam engines that were gaining popularity to drive farm equipment and river ships. Although he earned a hardly inspiring fifty cents a day, he loved machinery. By the time he had reached nineteen, he was working in the shop full time. Two years later he was as good a mechanic as his father. At this time, he plunked down three hundred sweat-earned dollars, gave his father an I.O.U. for eight hundred dollars more, and entered the business as a full partner.

Randy brought in fresh ideas. Whereas Olds and Son originally concentrated solely on repairing steam engines, young Olds invented a light steam engine that could power tools in shops and do many small yet indispensable farm chores such as wood sawing. These steam boilers were heated by a new substance called gasoline. Because they were such tremendous improvements over the bulky wood- and coal-consuming boilers, the demand for Olds' steam engine reached the point that by 1887 Olds and Son were manufacturing four-hundred engines a year. In addition, the company now began adapting its operations to do work on Otto gas engines used at this time mainly to power motorboats and water pumps. Thus Ransom became an expert on both steam and gasoline engines.

About this time, Olds thought he could build a steam engine suitable for driving a buggy. He actually put such a machine together—a half-dozen years before Duryea's Buggyaut. It ran, too, as Olds discovered when he took it out into the darkness for a trial. Its power was so weak, however, that it had to be hand pushed over a slight sidewalk grade. And it managed to chug for only a single block before its steam wheezed out. Randy continued to work three or four more years on the steamer before he concluded that the future lay with gasoline, not steam, engines. Nonetheless his three-wheeled steamer was not a bad little auto for the era, and Olds found a buyer for it—a rich man from India who used it in his native country for many years.

Now Olds turned to gasoline. By 1896 he was well along with his engine. Although he had no vehicle with which to enter the Chicago race of that year, he was a spectator as Duryea, Maxim, and the others slithered through the sleet and snow. Olds' own primitive horseless buggy was ready a few months later. This homemade auto was good enough to attract a few financial backers and on a warm day in 1897 they gave him the go-ahead to fix up a really first-rate car that could be sold commercially.

Olds soon completed his demonstration model. It was an odd-appearing contraption. Almost square, it had the engine high on a platform in the middle. There were cushions over the engine upon which four passengers could perch: two facing front and two facing back. Ransom was extremely proud of this first Oldsmobile (now on display in the Smithsonian Institution). A photo taken at the time shows Olds grasping the long steering lever with his left hand and the brake with his right. Behind him sits a pert, pretty young lady in a straw hat, probably his wife. We can only wonder where the couple and their friends were going on that shining day in a car that would remain forever young while they grew old.

Ransom had big car-making plans, intending to start right out with a stupendous production schedule that would turn out ten cars a week! But his first company, with funds of barely fifty thousand dollars, lacked the money to purchase the raw materials, the factory, and the machinery or to foot the prospective payroll. Because he felt he could never get the money he needed in smallish Lansing, Olds headed for the money market—New York City.

Although Olds had high hopes when he took the train to New York, it wasn't long before he learned, as he said, that "most people thought the car was just a toy." Bankers and wealthy individuals were skeptical of this novel car business. Why, they asked, would anyone want an oily, thunderclap-ping box on wheels to ride about town in when he could have

Ransom Olds and friends in one of his earliest creations, 1896.
(GENERAL MOTORS)

the comfort of a quiet, reliable horse-drawn hansom? And who would want an auto-thing for traveling long distances between cities? One need only look at that dirt-splattered, exhausted Maxim fellow (who had driven the first auto ever from Hartford to New York City a year earlier) to know that a horseless carriage could not compete with the luxury of a plush, clean railroad palace car. What was the future of automobiles? Only curiosity pieces for those fanatics who loved noise, dirt, and the self-punishment of rutted roads.

Olds spent ten days in New York trying to convince the businessmen and bankers that an auto company had a future. Finally he boarded the train for home. No one wanted to invest in him. They had passed up fortunes, but they didn't know it.

Olds went back to Detroit. There he managed to find a few men who would add their funds to the small amount he had received from those who had backed the construction of his demonstration model. On May 8, 1899, the Olds Motor Works was established with total funds of half-a-million dollars. Most of the money was put up by a wealthy Detroiter, Samuel Smith, who wanted to give his sons a present when they graduated from college. Smith, however, had no illusions about horseless carriages ever being much more than novelties. Smith assumed that Olds really knew this deep in his heart and that he would devote most of his time to expanding his already successful engine business. There was plenty of demand for stationary gas engines without putting them on wheels to be sent bouncing off into some quagmire.

Samuel Smith became president of Olds' company. He appointed his son, Fred, treasurer. He also presented Fred with the position of secretary. Olds had to settle for vice–president, with authority over production. Because the company was thus divided between the Smiths, who believed that future auto production should be aimed at the wealthy, and Olds, who believed in cheap cars for the ordinary wage earner, the seeds were sown for a dispute that would cause Olds to resign from his own company five years later. (At this time he would found a new concern, called REO, after Ransom E. Olds. REO was a huge success; it made Olds into one of the nation's wealthiest men; and it endures today as a major manufacturer of trucks.)

But the battle with the Smiths was not evident when the Olds Motor Works was founded in 1899. Ransom's main interest, at that time, was to plan many car models so that he and his backers could determine which one, or ones, would best suit the market. Olds and his staff started drawing plans for a wide variety of cars. No sooner was one blueprint completed, than they would begin on another. Some were for big cars, some for small. Some had gas engines, some electric. Some showed autos with the appearance of conventional horseless carriages, some showed autos with more radical lines. No one knew what a car should look like yet, for there had been no style trend yet established. Only one thing was certain: the buying public would not stand for a vehicle in which the motor was set in front of the steering wheel. That would be too radical. The proper place for the engine was tucked neatly out of sight under the seat.

As Olds' blueprints turned into completed cars, the company tried to sell them. But the public met each model with such indifference that by 1900 the Olds Motor Works had lost eighty-thousand dollars. This was nearly all of the firm's working capital—the rest of the original half-a-million dollars being tied up in machinery, payments on the factory, car parts, and workers' payrolls. The firm verged on bankruptcy.

Then, in the spring of 1901, Olds had a tremendous stroke of luck. His factory burned down.

Ransom was on the train going home from visiting his parents in California when the good fortune occurred. Arriving in Detroit, he read about the fire from a fellow traveler's newspaper.

Olds rushed to the destroyed factory. Amid the rubble, his manager told him there had been more than twenty cars almost ready for the market. But the fire swept through the plant with such rapidity that none of them could be saved. None, that is, except the little single-cylinder runabout with the curved dashboard. It had been standing near the door and was light enough to shove out in time. It was not much of a car, though; more a company mascot than a serious entry in the automobile field. The manager sighed. The damages ran to seventy-two thousand dollars and all that remained was the silly Curved Dash.

Ransom spent a sleepless night debating his future course. The company had almost no money and no good models from which to begin a new car line. What could he do?

Olds paced his bedroom. People saw him as a mild man. But beneath his calm exterior was a bedrock of determination. He vowed he would not accept defeat. If all that was left was the Curved Dash, then that was what he would produce. What did it matter if the thing had no top, no lights, no fenders! Olds had always believed that a cheap car could tap a vast market. Well, now he had a cheap car, let's see what would happen! He decided to commit the last of the company's reserve cash to manufacturing the Curved Dash. "I risked everything on the little car," he later confided.

Friends in Lansing helped Olds by donating the facilities of the state fairgrounds. In buildings still reeking of horses, pigs, and cattle, the Olds Motor Works resumed business. Ransom was the driving force in the company, which was virtually on the rocks. While he hired a labor force and arranged for the shipment of tools and supplies, he commuted between Lansing and Detroit to secure vital financial backing. Working day and night to save his sinking company, Olds suffered an illness that sent him to a hospital. But the gears he had spun continued to operate and within thirty days after the fire the first new Curved Dash was driven triumphantly up to Olds' hospital window. Ransom beamed at it. He quickly recovered.

There was still a long way for the struggling little company to go. The total car production was a microscopic three a week. At that rate, the company would never sell enough to meet its financial obligations. This slow production was particularly distressing in that the fire had given Olds such national publicity that purchase orders were starting to flow in from all over the country. Olds realized that what he had to do was not to double, or even triple, his production—not even raise it by ten times. He needed to produce thousands, not hundreds, of automobiles. This he must do quickly before both his cash ran out and the fickle public forgot about him. But how could he raise production when he had hardly enough money to pay for the three cars a week he was now turning out?

The answer, when it came to him in the summer of 1901, was astonishingly simple. He would let other companies make the various car parts and he would merely put them all together. That way he would not have to purchase more buildings, or more equipment, or pay the wages of more workers. He wouldn't have to pay for anything until the parts were delivered to his assembly plant.

For bodies and seat cushions, Olds selected Byron Everitt, who brought in Fred Fisher, eldest of the seven soon-to-be-famous Fisher brothers. To manufacture engines and transmissions, Olds farmed out a contract with the Dodge brothers, Horace and John, who would eventually become major car manufacturers themselves. When the Dodges, with their smallish shop, were unable to meet all his needs, Olds turned to Henry Leland, head of Detroit's top machine plant. Leland would one day soon become founder of the Cadillac Company. Although he didn't know it at the time, Olds was almost single-handedly creating the groundwork for Michigan's predominance in the automotive industry. Even a youngster named Henry Ford was an active observer at the Olds plant for a while.

Olds' plans astonished his associates, for he was letting out contracts that would obligate the company to assemble more than four thousand Curved Dash Oldsmobiles! This was equal to the total number of cars produced by all manufacturers in the entire country the year before! Influential persons in Lansing and Detroit buttonholed Olds to warn him that he was going to glut the market and ruin the business for everyone. Olds only shrugged and smiled in his quiet way. He was convinced one could probably not make too many inexpensive cars.

As his production began to increase, Olds realized that just to produce the saucy little Curved Dash was not enough. He must quickly create a dealer organization to enable him to display the car in towns and cities across the nation. But how should he convince prospective dealers to leave their blacksmith shops and bicycle stores and join up selling the new horseless carriages?

Olds pondered the problem. Then he remembered that Alexander Winton had astounded the nation by driving his car from Cleveland to New York City four years earlier. It was a feat that had been reported everywhere: imagine going to New York by car rather than by train! Winton had taken eleven days to plow across the horrible roads in Ohio, the upper corner of Pennsylvania, and New York State. But he had gained a huge amount of free publicity, which had been of immeasurable aid in helping him gain both dealers and sales.

Now, Olds thought, what if a Curved Dash made the even longer jaunt to New York City from Detroit. And what if this car—far cheaper than the Winton—could do it in less time! Wouldn't that make a fine news story. With such free publicity, it should be easy to attract car dealers into the Olds organization.

The plan, as it finally evolved, was for a driver to take a Curved Dash right as it came from the factory and to speed along the Canadian shore of Lake Erie. He would leap into the United States at Niagara, rip down New York's Mohawk Valley to Albany, and hurry south along the Hudson to New York City, arriving there to make a dramatic appearance at the National Auto Show, the second ever to be held.

Olds selected Roy Chapin for the vital task. In later life Chapin would cap a brilliant career by becoming Secretary of Commerce under President Herbert Hoover. But in 1901 he was just a footloose young man looking for adventure.

Olds was betting virtually his entire business on the success of the eight-hundred-mile trek. But, as he saw it, the whole auto industry was tossing marbles onto one big roulette wheel. Someone was going to strike the magic slot and make it big. Why not he?

On Tuesday, October 29, Chapin set out. He left with almost no fanfare, since Olds didn't dare publicize the trip until he was sure Chapin would not end up in a Canadian cow pasture. Crossing the Detroit River late in the afternoon, Chapin drove through the rustic Canadian countryside for fifty miles to Leamington. It is a shame Chapin did not keep a journal of this trip, for certainly the unexpected appearance of his odd-appearing machine created a sensation everywhere along his route. One can almost see him appearing suddenly like a visitor from another planet. For a moment, with the stuttering roar of his single piston and cloud of exhaust fumes, he would explode past a startled farmer. Then,

Roy Chapin arriving in N.Y. in 1901 in his Curved Dash Olds. (GENERAL MOTORS)

as quickly as he had come, he would be gone in a whirl of dust. Only the whinny of frightened horses would mark his passing.

Wednesday, October 30, was Chapin's finest day. The weather was autumn's most beautiful. The gravel road along Lake Erie was almost as hard and smooth as cement. Chapin let the accelerator out. Soon the Curved Dash was swooshing along the highway at 35 mph. Oak leaves—maroon and tawny brown—swirled behind. Although Chapin had to pause every few miles to refill his tires with air from a bicycle pump, by noon he had rumbled into London, Ontario, halfway through the Canadian segment of his journey. He had covered by then one hundred miles—fully three times the distance a horse-drawn buggy could have made in an entire day!

Chapin found a store where he could purchase gasoline. Then he headed his Curved Dash eastward once more. By 3 P.M. he had sped seventy-five additional miles. Pausing briefly to refuel in Brantford, he was quickly on the road again. His goal was St. Catherine's, beside Niagara Falls.

Chapin knew he was stretching things, for soon the sun was slanting low. Then there was a brilliant sunset and soon the lights of farmhouses began sparkling in the distance. Chapin stopped to light the pair of kerosene carriage lamps that hung on the car's front, more for decoration than illumination. As the twilight deepened, he continued on toward St. Catherine's. The bumping motion of the Olds combined with the feeble, flickering lamps made it impossible for Chapin to get a really good view of the road ahead.

Suddenly he rammed into a large stone. When he nervously climbed out of the car, he found his front axle as bent as a swayback nag.

From his toolbox, Chapin fished out a hammer and pounded

the axle into a halfway operable condition. Then, with his wheels wobbling wildly, he made his way cautiously to St. Catherine's. It had been a near catastrophe, for had the axle broken, the entire trip might well have been scratched.

That night Chapin dispatched a telegram to his boss, who had taken a train to New York City. Olds could not believe what he read. His driver was at Niagara Falls? Could it be that he had made a distance of 278 miles in a single day? Olds was convinced that Chapin was either lost or the rocky roads had jarred his brain loose.

The next day was Halloween. Chapin and his Curved Dash chugged across the suspension bridge spanning the Niagara River. Soon he was making his way down rutted American roads. Now his cylinder gasket began blowing out every time he gunned the Curved Dash up an extra-steep hill. To replace a gasket was not difficult, but it was time consuming. By the time he reached Rochester, New York, he was so exhausted that he could go no further. He had covered only eighty-five miles, but he was certain that with some rest he could make up the loss on the next day.

Early on Friday, November 1—his fourth day since leaving Detroit—Chapin was again on his way. It was much tougher now, for there had been rain and the hilly dirt road was very slippery. To make driving even worse, the bent axle caused the car to wobble and skid nearly beyond control. It was all Chapin could to do keep from plunging into a ditch. Nevertheless, he managed to slide seventy-five miles to Syracuse, which he reached by noon.

At Syracuse, Chapin talked to some teamsters who had recently driven their freight wagons from the east. Every one of them was discouraging about Chapin's chances of making it to Albany. Dark rain clouds had constantly deluged them while turning the roads into all but impossible swamps. Chapin went to a small eating spot where he debated what to do. Somehow he had to reach New York City in time for the Auto Show. Then, in a moment of brilliance, he had a solution. Hurrying out of the cafe, he leaped into the Olds and sped off.

In a few moments, Chapin reached the Erie Canal, which connected Albany with the Great Lakes. He knew the canal boats were pulled by mules trudging along a raised towpath. Although wagons, with their iron-rimmed wheels, were strictly prohibited from the towpath, informants told Chapin that doctors and other persons could use the path in emergencies. What could be more of an emergency, Chapin mused, than saving the Oldsmobile Company. Without further hesitation, he gunned his Curved Dash up the towpath embankment. Then he was off.

Chapin drove for some time before meeting his first barge. Almost as soon as the mules heard Chapin's engine, they became unmanageable. Even when Chapin quietly parked at the side of the path, the unruly mules would not go by. At last the enraged driver ordered him to inch slowly along the canal side.

As Chapin continued east, he must have been impressed by the irony of the occasion. Here he was in the machine of the future. Yet there was no suitable highway for him except this ancient mule-way built back in the days when the United States stopped at the Rockies and California was a foreign country.

Chapin opened up his trusty Olds as far as he dared, praying the bent axle would not buckle. Down the muddy, but level, towpath the little car spurted, sending jets of water spinning into his face from the unfendered wheels. By evening, Chapin had left Rochester 145 miles behind and was within 200 miles of New York City, where Ransom Olds was sweating out the days.

On Saturday, Chapin chugged past the imposing state capitol in Albany. Then he turned south down the scenic Hudson Valley, where soft hills outlined his route. Late that afternoon he reached a railway express office where a front axle shipped from Detroit awaited him. Loading the precious piece onto his car, he located a machine shop where a mechanic replaced the old axle bent outside Niagara with the new one.

On the following morning, Sunday, Chapin set out on what he believed would be the last leg of his epic journey to New York City. But, as the Oldsmobile climbed the Hudson hills, growls in the transmission warned Chapin that all was not right. As the motor's agony increased, Chapin realized that the transmission was completely shot. He was barely able to stagger into the town of Peekskill before the transmission gave out entirely. He had hoped to be in New York City, which was only forty-five miles away, by that evening. That would have enabled the Curved Dash to be put on display at the Auto Show Monday morning. Instead, he had to spend all day Monday fitting parts and pieces into the transmission. As Chapin told Ransom Olds the bad news over a scratchy line of those new things called telephones, he noticed how worried his boss sounded.

Chapin got up before the roosters on Tuesday. The engine hummed as he drove down the Hudson Valley. Soon he spotted the distant spires of New York's churches. By 9:30 he was in the city itself. He turned down Fifth Avenue and could see the Waldorf Astoria Hotel just a few blocks ahead. Olds was nervously waiting for him in the lobby. Yet at that instant, when the trip was almost over, a pedestrian stepped

into the street in front of the Curved Dash. Frantically
Chapin jerked the steering lever to one side. The car swerved
out of control. With a sickening crunch a rear wheel smashed
against the stone curb and the car lurched to a stop.

Chapin jumped down to the pavement. He was shaken
and distressed. The wheel frame was horribly bent and several wire spokes were broken. Yet he was ready for such an
emergency, for he had been making repairs to the car every
half hour since leaving Deroit. Chapin hammered the frame
until it was relatively straight and replaced the spokes. Then
he cranked up the engine. A few minutes later he was in
front of the Waldorf.

The hotel doorman eyed Chapin suspiciously. The fact
that he had just completed the longest motorcar trip ever
taken in the United States did not impress the crisp doorman.
All he cared about was that the young man was covered
with grease and dirt. No one could enter New York's fanci-
est hotel looking like that! Chapin was sent to the rear to
use the servants' entrance.

Once the muck-matted Curved Dash was cleaned up, Olds
put it on display. Although show visitors gaped at this seemingly frail little machine that had made the unimaginable
journey from Detroit, officials of the Spaulding Company,
who had agreed to market the car in New York City, could
not convince themselves that the Curved Dash would ever
really compete with the larger cars. As the manufacturers of
nationally known sporting goods, the Spaulding officials were
convinced they were far wiser in the business world than this
dreamy Ransom somebody from Michigan. Spaulding had
agreed to order one hundred Curved Dashes, but, the company had now concluded that such an order was ridiculous,
for it represented 10 percent of all the cars then owned in

the entire city. The show had hardly begun before a starchy Spaulding representative informed Olds that his company was going to cancel the arrangement.

Olds had counted on Spaulding's prestige to help him attract dealers in other cities. But what could he do if the company simply refused to honor the agreement? Making the best of it, Olds told the Spaulding officials that they could back out if they would just permit him to keep their sign on display with the Curved Dash so other prospective dealers would believe Spaulding had faith in the car. Spaulding agreed to the rather unethical procedure. By this act, Spaulding probably saved the future of the Oldsmobile Company.

Zero hour was now approaching for the optimist from Detroit. It was vital that Olds not leave the Auto Show without lining up some agents to market his cars. But it was almost the end of the week and he was still without an agent in New York, the nation's largest city and center of the news media on which he depended for favorable national publicity.

Then it happened. A flashy man named Ray Owen approached Olds. Owen had sold Olds cars in Cleveland and thought he could do the job in New York. Olds kept calm. Apparently unruffled, he told Owen and his partner, Roy Rainey, that he might consider their request providing they would agree to take not the one hundred cars that Spaulding had considered impossible, but five hundred. The two men glanced nervously at each other. They, too, knew that in the entire city there were only one thousand cars. Yet they had confidence in the pert little machine as well as in their own peculiar methods of promotion. They told Olds to come to their room and work out a firm agreement.

As Olds walked through the Waldorf halls, a little motor churned in his head. Upon entering the partners' hotel room, Olds made a dramatic decision. "Gentlemen," he said, "it isn't my business but I would like to see you two put this thing over in a big way. I would like to see you make this order for a thousand cars. Then the public would drop its jaw and take notice."

Owen and Rainey must have gulped. Did this man have a piston loose? Sell a thousand cars in a single year in a single city from a single agency? But it would make news—would it make news! With trembling fingers, the partners signed the contract.

Newspapers carried word of the fantastic agreement throughout the country, and soon everyone was talking about it: a thousand cars . . . outfit named Oldsmobile . . . fellows whose factory burned down about half a year ago . . . that's the car that drove 'cross near half the country a mite ago . . . only costs $650.

While orders began to flood into Lansing, Owen and Rainey engaged in a variety of publicity stunts that astounded New York and intrigued the nation. Hardly a day passed but what the madcap dealers weren't roaring along city streets in their Curved Dashes scaring horses, kicking up dust, and generally making spectacles of themselves. They actually liked being arrested for speeding, since it proved the little cars could compete with the fast expensive ones. Even more newsworthy were the times they gently bumped policemen off their patrol bikes.

The dazzle-brained antics paid off. The Curved Dash quickly acquired a reputation of sauciness that put it in a class over the ponderous Wintons, Haynes-Appersons, or Pope-Toledos. Perhaps the capstone of the partners' success came when none other than Chauncey Depew, president of the mighty New York Central Railroad system, allowed Owen to publicize a photograph of him taken as he and his Curved Dash rode in magnificent dignity to work.

Curved Dash sales began to climb in New York City. Soon the little car ensnared the hearts of otherwise cynical New Yorkers. News of this spread to people in other cities. To spin about in a Curved Dash became the smart thing to do.

Olds had done the almost impossible: he had turned a lowly shop reject into America's first automotive darling. It was an accomplishment that brought him pride and satisfaction for the remainder of his long and illustrious life.

6

"It Must Be Great To Be Crazy And Ride Around in an Automobile"

Silence fell over the Oldsmobile plant. Machinery ground to a halt. Conveyor belts whirred slower and then stopped. Soon the only sound was that of workers shuffling off their jobs.

The men gathered around the end of the assembly line. They whispered excitedly among themselves, for this was a great moment. The whispering quieted as one of the men climbed into the car at the end of the line. After another worker cranked the car into life, the first man drove it carefully out the factory door.

The men broke into wild cheering. They tossed their caps into the air. The factory whistle screamed. Everywhere there was bedlam. The reason: Olds had just assembled his two thousandth car. He had overtaken the industry leader, Colonel Pope, and his best-selling electric model.

Ransom Olds, looking like a shy professor in his eyeglasses, was there to be honored by his workers. The highlight of the ceremony was the presentation to Olds of a handsome watch chain pendant in the shape of a Curved Dash Olds. It had been paid for by the workers themselves. Olds received it bursting with pride. Forevermore, it would be one of his most cherished possessions.

Despite the fact that during this vintage year of 1902 Olds ultimately topped twenty-five hundred in car sales, he was determined to better that mark during the following twelve months. Four thousand cars was his goal for 1903!

With this figure before him, Olds began advertising his sporty car in the widely read *Saturday Evening Post* magazine. One ad told readers that the Oldsmobile was unquestionably "the best thing on wheels." Another sang out to drivers that the Curved Dash was so perfect that, once behind the wheel, they would have "nothing to watch but the road." Through Olds' adept use of advertising, passion to own a Curved Dash became so strong that one lady asserted that she "might just as well be out of the world as without an Oldsmobile." Never before had auto manufacturers used advertising to such effect.

Ransom was also quick to realize the value of publicity stunts. The Detroit to New York trip had shown him the attention an endurance run could command. With this in mind, he hit upon the ultimate: a cross-country expedition from California to New York. Accordingly, a Curved Dash was shipped to San Francisco, and on July 6, 1903, Eugene Hammond and L. L. Whitman began their epic transcontinental venture.

For nearly two and a half months the two men jerked and jostled along country byways. Up the Rockies they chugged, passing sheepmen who had never heard of—much less seen—

a horseless carriage. During one stretch of nine hundred miles they drove without meeting another car. Sometimes they traveled on traces that were not roads at all, their only guide being the sun and stray signposts planted at favored crossroads. Mechanical problems were numerous, but they solved them with hammer and luck. Crossing the Great Plains, their tires became sieved with holes. Hoping oats would plug the punctures, they filled their tires with the grain and continued on undaunted. "I believe I planted the whole state of Nebraska with oats that fell out as we went along," Hammond was to quip.

On September 7, the drivers sputtered into Detroit. After a Caesar's welcome from Olds, they were off for New York. Ten days later they made it. Despite the fact that the Curved Dash was the third car to thus commemorate the one-hundredth anniversary of Lewis and Clark's departure for the West, the Olds earned gallons of fame because the little car made it from coast to coast on just a single cylinder.

Soon celebrities everywhere were driving the Curved Dash. The Queen of England bounced about London in her chauffeur-driven Curved Dash. The Queen of Italy likewise rode along highways that had once heard the sounds of Roman chariots. Mark Twain loved the little car and wrote about it. Sir Thomas Lipton, of tea fame, boasted about his Curved Dash and the pleasures of motoring. Even the gruff baronial Krupp family in Germany were seen about their vast Ruhr steel mills in spanking new Curved Dashes.

For speed buffs, Olds sent his little car racing to stupendous records. Before the end of 1903 an Oldsmobile driven by daredevil E. R. Thomas attained the legendary speed of a mile a minute—sixty miles an hour. America gasped.

About this time, songwriter Gus Edwards collaborated with Vincent Bryan in writing "My Merry Oldsmobile," which

The Curved Dashes set out on the first transcontinental race, 1905.
(GENERAL MOTORS)

sparked into instant success. Soon nearly everyone was singing or whistling "Come away with me Lucile," as, in their merry Oldsmobile, they glided down elm-shaded byways.

The climax in the career of the jolly Curved Dash came in 1905, when James Abbott of the U.S. Office of Public Roads proposed that two of the popular cars actually race across the entire continent from New York City to Portland, Oregon. The winner would receive five thousand dollars, and it was hoped he would arrive in Portland on or near June 20 the opening day of the National Good Roads Convention. Abbott felt sure that the race would publicize the horrible condition of United States highways and the need for government action in that area.

When the race was announced, many persons protested that the June 20 convention date was far too early, for blinding snow storms could still be encountered in the Rockies when the drivers would be entering them in late spring. But the officials said the date was firm and the drivers would just have to chance the hazards.

Despite the dangers, two experienced drivers accepted the challenge, and on May 8, 1905, Dwight Huss and Percy McGargel, along with a codriver for each, climbed into Curved Dashes, gunned their single-cylinder engines, and took off. A crowd of well-wishers yelled encouragement as the two buggies chugged slowly down New York's bumpy streets. To most persons watching, it seemed as if the little vehicles were very unlikely conquerors of three thousand rutted miles of road that rocked through blistering deserts and mountain mazes.

The initial leg of the route led north 160 miles up the Hudson Valley to Albany. The roadway was brightened by sunshine as the cars sputtered along. "Our spirits were high and the way looked easy," Huss wrote lyrically. But the day

EASTERN HALF OF THE CURVED DASH RACE - 1905

was too bright, and by the time they had reached Albany that evening each of the four smarted under a crackling sunburn.

As the racers slept that night, torrential rain doused upper New York State. When they took to the road the next morning it was little more than one long swamp. What with the publicity accompanying them, they were unable to follow Roy Chapin's more favored route along the Erie Canal towpath. "We were soon covered from head to foot with mire," wrote McGargel, "while our baggage and supplies, strapped on the rear deck, were almost unrecognizable."

Although Old Steady, as McGargel's car had been christened, could proceed at only a frog's pace, it was enough to frighten most beasts and natives encountered on the way. The usual response of the startled buggy driver was for him to turn into a field, where he could safely wait for the growling contraption to bump past him. However, one pretty young girl driving a milk wagon refused to be intimidated. She grasped the reins firmly, whipped her two horses, and galloped triumphantly past Old Steady. McGargel was impressed and left a delightful sketch of this young miss in the memoirs he was writing of his trip.

Both Old Steady and Old Scout, Huss's vehicle, received fresh-water baths at Syracuse that evening, while the two pairs of racers joked about their experiences. Despite the mud, they had made 150 miles that day. To reach Portland by June 20, they had to average just 90 miles per day, so they were well ahead of schedule.

By 6 A.M. the next morning both Curved Dashes were heading westward toward Buffalo. Trains of the New York Central Railroad—in which passengers could reach Chicago from New York in easy luxury in half the time it had taken McGargel and Huss just to splatter to Syracuse—sped past them. Only the most eccentric prophet would have dared predict that the unsightly and uncomfortable auto would eventually put most passenger train lines virtually out of business.

While the trains rumbled on, the two cars sloshed westward down the road-swamp. At last they reached Buffalo, where the drivers were treated to a fine banquet by the owner of the local Oldsmobile agency. Then the four men set out for Erie, Pennsylvania. But the carelessly posted direction signs confused them. McGargel would write:

> As usual both crews lost themselves and traveled many more miles than were necessary. In fact, after making numerous turns, Old Steady struck a section of the country where automobiles appeared to be unknown. A small boy on his way to school, whom we stopped to ask about the road, was frightened and commenced to cry violently.

Soon after, a girl, after taking one look at the begoggled, mud-covered tourists, gave a yell and started down the road at top speed. When she saw we were overtaking her she made for the side fields, falling several times before she finally convinced herself that we were not really after her. The next youth we met dived bodily through a barbed-wire fence and streaked across the fields.

Although it was nearly as difficult to ask directions as to find the road to Erie, both cars managed to thread the labyrinth of cowpaths and mud traces that linked the town with the countryside.

They continued westward. By May 12, Old Steady was passing Old Scout in Cleveland, McGargel giving a good-natured raspberry to Huss, who was loading up with gas from an Olds dealer. Through the low-lying portions of Ohio they plowed, sometimes running for a quarter mile without seeing the roadway through the sheet of water that gurgled up to their axles.

Seven days after leaving New York City they were in Chicago. With a quarter of the way to Portland now covered and with the target date of June 20 still five weeks away, the drivers felt they would reach their goal ahead of schedule, even though the forbidding Rockies had yet to be crossed. They were running neck and neck, and the five thousand dollars was still up for grabs.

Out of Chicago they entered lush prairies where spring rains had turned the rich black soil into a gooey gumbo.

The mud all day has been that sticky, thick black mud that only Illinois . . . can boast of. To get through it, we were obliged on several occasions to use block and tackle. . . . [Once] every one of the four wheels was so stuck up with mud as to render the spokes invisible. The cars and occupants were so covered with mud when we arrived [in Davenport, Iowa] tonight that we were hardly recognizable.

After crossing the Mississippi, the roads were more to their liking—at least for a while. Both drivers opened their throttles and soon the Curved Dashes were skimming over the yellow clay at up to twenty miles an hour. But the farther west they traveled into the drier climate, the more they were bothered by sun-hardened ruts. It wasn't long before they were complaining of the violent jolting which left their tailbones punching their necks. In addition, the cars still carried such a heavy caking of Illinois mud that the radiator coils failed to cool the engine. As steam billowed upward, the drivers had to crawl under the car and spend a full hour picking out the mud with a screwdriver.

Moving into central Iowa, McGargel and Bart Stanchfield, his codriver, met an irritated farmer who snapped at them for terrifying his horses with a car from New York. "Do you know the law in this state compels you fellows to run your machine into a field until we can pass by?" he stormed. When McGargel and Stanchfield protested that they had never heard of such a requirement, the farmer raised his fists and shouted he would lick them both here and now.

With that the two merrily sped off, leaving the fuming farmer and his nervous team spitting dust. They continued down the hacked-up road until they reached a stream where the bridge was down. As this was almost an hourly event, they were ready with their trusty block and tackle to pull Old Steady through the soft river bed to the opposite shore. Fortunately, they were off again before the angry farmer caught up with them.

Not all Iowans were antiautos. Wherever Old Steady or

Old Scout stopped, the drivers were quickly surrounded by friendly, curious natives, asking how their flimsy thing could hope to cross the Rockies. Many natives were not impressed with the autos. In fact, to quite a few it seemed as if cars were more a throwback to the past than instruments of the future. McGargel remembered one motherly lady who paused beside him as he sweated over a repair. She stared at his dust-stained face, then scrutinized the temporarily useless pile of

Huss fords a stream in the transcontinental race, 1905. (GENERAL MOTORS)

mud and machinery beside him. Sympathy softened her Iowa-hardened jaw. "You poor fellows," she said sadly, "I am awfully sorry for you." Then she went off in her wagon, which moved with a simple "giddap" and made every hill without blowing a single gasket.

The grooved, bony roads were devilish on the cars' rubber and canvas tires. On May 20, the travelers did only seventy-two miles, what with the endless flats. It seemed as if they could hardly shimmy over a rut without causing that hated hiss of escaping tire-air. Then came the wobbly stop, the up and down of the jack, the tire patch, and the shoulder-aching hand pumping to refill the tire. Yet they managed to hobble through Des Moines and by May 22 were crossing western Iowa. Now the roadway was often blocked with herds of pigs, causing the drivers to clamp on their horns.

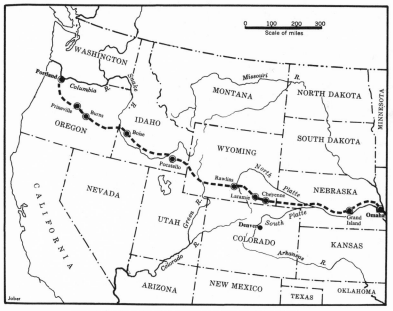

WESTERN HALF OF THE CURVED DASH RACE - 1905

By the afternoon of May 23, the two vehicles, running within a few miles of one another, were approaching Omaha. It was here that they passed the first machine they had seen working on the Iowa roads. It was such an unusual event— this feeble attempt to improve the highway—that McGargel made special note of it in his journal.

Omaha was a name to quicken the pulse. It meant they were halfway across the country—and it had taken only fifteen days.

Just upriver from Omaha were the bluffs where Lewis and Clark had held council with Indians a hundred years earlier. It had taken the explorers from 1803 to 1806 to lead their vigorous band of two dozen from the Missouri frontier to the Pacific and back. The Curved Dash race was part of the four-year Lewis and Clark commemoration. Beginning at Omaha, Scout and Steady would be, in a general way, retracing the westward progression of the expedition. But more than reliving history, they were making history of their own.

In 1905, as in the time of Lewis and Clark, the Missouri marked the beginning of the frontier. As Huss, McGargel, and their two companions strapped on 38–caliber revolvers, they recalled that it had been less than thirty years since the Sioux and Cheyenne had wiped out Custer. Although the Indians were now largely confined to reservations, the West still had a reputation for lawlessness. The empty spaces were wide and many, and the towns few and far between.

But none of the men were chilled by the prospect before them. They were receiving such nationwide publicity that town officials along their route were well alerted for their arrival. Furthermore, they would be traveling for the most part on roadways beside the Union Pacific Railroad. Jim Abbott, the U.S. Public Roads official who had inaugurated the race, would be traveling parallel to them to tend to their personal and automotive needs.

"The boys pulled out of Omaha on a balmy, beautiful afternoon with high hopes and cheering prospects," Abbott recalled. "With roads as they expected to find them, Cheyenne, 500 miles away, should easily have been reached in three days. There were neither heavy grades nor deep sand to impede progress."

The road was, in fact, the ancient Oregon Trail, one-time prairie schooner thoroughfare to the Pacific. During its heyday in the 1840s and 1850s it was not unusual for six hundred or more covered wagons to pass outposts along the trail in a single day. With the land flat to gently rolling, the wagons could rumble across the Great Plains grasslands with ease, making between twenty and twenty-five miles on a good day. Although skies were almost always cloudless in Nebraska, water was readily available from the Platte River, which the Trail followed closely (as did the more modern Union Pacific).

The boys, as Abbott called them, were not as lucky as most Oregon Trail emigrants. They found themselves driving through constant spring rainstorms that soaked through seams in their rubber raincoats and left the roadway an impossible mire. They had no choice except to make their own road by driving along the crest of the low hills that rippled over the prairie. "They seesawed from ridge to ridge," Abbott recalled, "and back and forth across the Platte River," which, although it was up to a quarter mile wide at some points, was usually so shallow that the water barely ran over the cars' hubcaps.

In addition to the Platte, there were many small creeks to cross. Sometimes it was preferable to drive right through the water than chance taking a bridge. McGargel learned the danger of bridges when, upon approaching Grand Island, Nebraska, Old Steady crashed through a rotten bridge floor, thudded against the creek bottom, and badly bent both the front and rear axles. Although McGargel managed to hobble fifteen miles to town, by the time he had the car workable, Old Scout was forty miles ahead.

The next day was equally difficult and neither car could make much more than fifty miles. They were now moving across "mudholes, buffalo wallows and alkali pits that seemed impossible for any automobile to force its way through" (to quote from McGargel's journal). At this point they were averaging just five miles an hour, actually less than the horse-drawn vehicles the automobile was designed to replace.

Despite the disappointing progress, the men were intrigued by the billowing prairie world through which they were slowly traversing:

Game is very abundant all through Nebraska, jack rabbits and cottontails being seen by the score, while quail, wild doves, prairie chickens, and many large birds with which I am not familiar [this is McGargel writing], are found in numbers. . . . We repeatedly ran through prairie dog villages, comprised of from two to five hundred mounds. The dogs [actually a species of rodent related to the ground squirrel] would congregate on the tops of their houses until Old Steady would be almost upon them, when they would scamper down into the regions below.

There were more dangerous animals, too. Wolves lurked in the distance, not bothering the motorists, but killing cattle and horses. At night, coyotes howled weird, chilling cadences that kept McGargel and Stanchfield awake in their hotel rooms (the men classified themselves as tourists, not outdoor campers). Rattlesnakes lurked in the brush, and McGargel killed one with his 38 that measured more than six feet. The rattlers were so numerous that it was often a peril to leave the car. (Even so, the boys had no experience to compare with that of explorer Meriwether Lewis, who, in 1805, was chased eighty yards by a charging bear, and escaped only by plunging into an icy stream.)

Once in a while, the drivers passed a herd of cattle accompanied by cowboys, who waved at them. But usually there were no living creatures, man or animal, to break the expanse of grass that extended halfway to infinity. It was this deep solitude that differentiated the Great Plains from the past. How different was the living landscape as viewed by Horace Greeley a bare five decades earlier:

> I would rather not bore the public with buffalo. . . . All day yesterday, they darkened the earth around us, often seeming to be drawn up like an army in battle array on the ridges and down their slopes a mile or so. . . . What strikes the stranger with most amazement is their immense numbers. I know a million is a great many, but I am confident we saw that number yesterday. . . . Often the country for miles on either hand seemed quite black with them.

Now they were gone—quite gone. All that remained was the wallows where they once caked themselves for protection against flies and the grooved paths that had led from one feeding ground to another.

The two Olds putt-putted uneventfully across the unnaturally quiet Nebraska plains. On the last day of May Old Scout crossed the Wyoming line and Dwight Huss and Milford Wigle, his codriver, received an enthusiastic reception in Cheyenne. (Old Steady rolled in twenty-four hours later.) Without a pause both hurried on, for they were eleven days behind schedule and the most rugged portion of their trek lay immediately ahead.

By the time the boys reached Laramie, over a hacked-up but passable sixty mile drive from Cheyenne, the first snow-tipped outriders of the Rocky Mountains hunched menacingly above the horizon. Huss and Wigle left Laramie at eight on the morning of June 2. They skirted Elk Mountain, driving in a northwesterly direction, and by seven that evening had reached the hamlet of Medicine Bow. From here a dirt pathway turned toward a low pass. They were barely out of Medicine Bow when Old Scout struck a sinkhole. Sandy ooze rose around the car until it sank almost out of sight. With the aid of their trusty block and tackle, and the broad back of a native, they managed to pull the car out. But it was not in running condition and they left it alone in the night while they found makeshift beds in the village.

The next morning Old Scout was coaxed into working and the two men continued onward. As they entered the mountains, the streams grew more rapid. There were no bridges in this wilderness, little traveled since the completion of the Union Pacific Railroad had put the Oregon Trail out of business. The road was far worse than when the prairie schooners had flattened the bristling sagebrush into something passable. "I don't know how Old Scout ever lived through it," Huss recalled, "but she did. We forded five big creeks, driving over rocks and stones. And [there was so] much sagebrush that Old Scout's radiator looked like a badly twisted piece of tin."

Trailing behind Huss by sixty or seventy miles, McGargel and Stanchfield were being plagued by their own troubles. They had left Laramie forgetting to stop at the Union Pacific station for their consignment of motor oil. The oil they purchased at a ramshackle general store farther down the route had eventually congealed to a consistency of chewing

Fixing a flat, 1905. (GENERAL MOTORS)

gum. McGargel had to trudge five miles across cobbles and cactus to Rawlings, where he hired a horse team to have Old Steady dragged to town for cleaning.

Out of Rawlings, the hard-luck duo entered the Great Divide Basin, "a stretch of sandy country," ran McGargel's journal, "in which absolutely nothing can grow except sage-brush, greasewood, and cactus. There were no ranches, cattle, or horses for many miles, and, in fact, hardly any living thing at all except jackrabbits, prairie dogs, and rattlesnakes. Water was very scarce. . . ." There was virtually no road at all, only the merest trace over the sun-seared red and white sand.

Sometimes Old Steady's rear wheels would sink in the powdery sand nearly up to the axles. Nevertheless, McGargel and Stanchfield managed to cover a hundred miles that torrid day, crossing the Continental Divide and eventually staggering into the tiny railroad town of Point of Rocks, Wyoming, at 9:30 P.M.

After sleeping in the Union Pacific freight house, they were back on the so-called road early the next morning. They made only seventy miles that day through the blistering desert, but much time was spent fording the turbulent Green River. Leaving the dusty hamlet of Granger at dawn the following morning, they were suddenly caught in one of those fierce Rocky Mountain storms that seem to materialize from nothing. Thunder banged about them. The sky grew dark as charcoal. Then a barrage of hail hurled down upon them.

The boys leaped from their exposed car seats and wiggled beneath the car to save themselves, for the hailstones were as large as baseballs. But then the hail was joined by rain, which turned the ground upon which they lay into a muddy bathtub.

After what seemed a soggy eternity, the two slithered out from under the car and attempted to continue westward. It wasn't long, however, before they found their way barred by a swollen creek. The churning water made it impossible to determine how deep the creek was. After hesitating, the boys decided they could not afford to wait for the water to subside, since they were already more than a day behind Old Scout. So they nervously nosed their Olds down the creek bank.

As they inched through the swirling water, they found themselves going deeper and deeper until the torrent reached Old Steady's hubcaps. A few feet farther on and Steady's wheels had almost disappeared. By the time they were halfway across, water was bubbling through the floorboard. With that, the engine coughed out.

Stranded in midstream, Old Steady rocked with the current and began sinking into the sandy creek bottom. Bart and Percy jumped into the icy mountain water and tried to push the car forward. But, with the creek rampaging about their waists, they could get no traction. In despair, they half stumbled, half swam to shore. There they watched, while the storm rumbled in the mountains around them and the creek kept rising until all that remained of their gallant little Curved Dash was the top of the seat.

The two men waited dejectedly several hours for the water to go down. Finally they realized that by this time Old Steady was so loaded with mud, sand, and silt that nothing except a team of horses could get her out. Sighting a rundown shanty in the distance, they hiked to it for aid.

The house was made of logs crudely chinked with mud. As they pushed the door open, the foul odor of pigs wafted over them. After a quick glance around the littered interior showed them that the owner was not there, they walked to the barn, which, if possible, was even more disreputable than the cabin. There they found a grizzled old sheepman waiting for them with a loaded shotgun.

Lone John, the sheepman, was a tough man who had just been released from jail for cutting open the head of a neighbor with an axe. He hankered for some talk, however, and laid aside his gun while he talked. After listening to Lone recite his troubles, McGargel finally got him to bring a team down to the creek. A line was hooked to still-submerged Old Steady. Then, Lone John put the whip to his string of mustangs and slowly dragged the car out of the coffee-colored water.

It took the two drivers several tedious hours to remove the debris from the engine, which had to be virtually taken apart. But at last the car coughed into life and McGargel steered her out of Lone John's garbage bin and down a long canyon in the Absaroka Range toward Idaho.

Once in Idaho, mountains closed even closer about them. Glaciers lapped at them with long, frosty tongues. The drivers now were so high that their breath came with difficulty in the atmosphere of rarified oxygen. Once, when McGargel was pumping up a tire after one of their many blowouts, he suffered a violent nosebleed caused by the exertion and the thin atmospheric pressure.

Both cars met their first Indians not far from Pocatello. They were members of the Shoshone tribe, one time lords of the northern Rockies. Shoshone forefathers had provided Lewis and Clark with vital aid exactly a hundred years earlier. The explorers had held council with the powerful tribesmen, had smoked the sacred peace pipe with them, had feasted on Shoshone meat, and had been entertained by Indian dancers for one entire night. The Shoshones had traded the Americans horses to help them carry their supplies over the rugged mountains, and Clark had promised to reward them for their trouble. Now, a century later, the drivers saw what rewards the Indians had received: they had been reduced from the proud people who had befriended Lewis and Clark to beggars and petty thieves who were nuisances to the white folk who had taken their ancestoral lands.

Huss was banging out the miles far more rapidly than McGargel. On June 10 he and Mil Wigle rolled into Boise, where a big delegation met them with cheers, a fine banquet, and some homemade keys to the city. Huss sniffled through the festivities, for he was suffering from a severe cold picked up riding through a cloudburst in their open car three days earlier. Indeed, both men were so exhausted from their pace-setting journey (which had by now bumped and battered them for more than a solid month) that they spent four days in Boise recuperating.

On June 15, Huss paid fifty cents to be ferried over the swift-moving Snake River. Then he drove Old Scout down the boat ramp and onto the soil of Oregon. The last leg of the race had begun.

The road lay over a route currently followed by U.S. Highway 20. It was almost deserted country, with rocky pinnacles and ancient lava beds that glistened darkly in the sun. The boys had been warned about the scorpions abounding in the boulders, so they were nervous whenever they had to stop for water or car adjustments. But the road itself was surprisingly good and they sped westward.

At the townlet of Burns they made their last contact with the Union Pacific, their vital supply line. Then, for more than a hundred miles of desolate desert, they were completely on their own. Pushing through the rocks and sand in the open little car was an experience never to be forgotten. They were dependent on Old Scout for almost everything. Should the single-cylinder engine decide to quit, they would be stranded in a bleak region where water was scarce and food non-existent. But the faithful Curved Dash kept firing, and they made it to Prineville, where a pair of lady photographers, eager to win the prize offered by Ransom Olds, snapped their pictures.

Although they were now virtually in sight of Portland, the most perilous portion of the entire trip lay just ahead. This was the dreaded Cascade Mountain Range. If they could just manage to cross the range without smashing their car, they would easily beat McGargel, who was several hundred miles behind them. They could also reach Portland in time to make the Good Roads Convention. But one accident might lay up the car long enough for McGargel to pass them, as well as prevent them from attending the convention.

An hour out of Prineville they spotted the three snow-etched peaks of the Sisters Mountains sawing upward before them. The road up the pass was of a soft sand base, the very worst sort for climbing. Old Scout groaned and strained as she labored up the steep switchbacks. At times Huss thought the rod or one of the gears would crack under the tremendous pressure. Pines and firs barely moved past them as the little car valiantly climbed higher and higher. The wind grew chill and the trees gave way to scrub growths.

At last they reached the summit of Santiam Pass. They paused on the wind-whipped plateau, savoring the thrill of conquest. They thought victory was as good as theirs.

But going down Santiam, Old Scout's brakes started burning up. Bouncing down the dipping road, they found brake smoke and the distressing odor of smoldering rubber trailed behind. As Huss frantically wrestled with the steering, Wigle tried to slow the car by hanging onto the rear bumper. But the brakes continued to sizzle and gradually the car lurched ahead faster and faster. Soon the brakes were gone completely. With Wigle hanging on desperately, Old Scout hurled down the mountainside almost out of control. On one side of them was a rocky canyon several hundred feet deep. Closer and closer Old Scout lurched toward the deadly precipice. Huss worked desperately with the steering lever. Only his supreme skill enabled them to miss hurtling over the canyon edge.

After seven wild, uncontrollable miles, Old Scout finally came to rest at the foot of the mountain. Huss and Wigle mopped their brows and gasped for breath. They had been

warned not to go down the mountain without a boulder tied
to the rear of the car to aid the brakes. Now they knew why.

After they regained control of their nerves, the two men
drove on to the hamlet of Lebanon. The next morning, June
20, they reached Oregon City, where they were met by a
delegation of Portland auto enthusiasts. The Portland
crowd gave them a wild escort to their city, where the streets
were thronged with persons wishing to see this amazing auto
and the daredevil drivers who had crossed the entire continent
in just forty-four days! They had actually arrived in Portland
on the very day, and within an hour, of the opening of the
Good Roads Convention!

At one that afternoon, Huss proudly drove to the convention hall, where he delivered a message to the congregation
from the governor of Michigan. That evening the Portland
Auto Club had a parade through the city with Old Scout
cruising illustriously at the head of the line.

When McGargel and Stanchfield rolled into Portland a
week later, they found Old Scout and her drivers celebrities.
Even the faded caps worn by the victors were on exhibition
at a local hat store. Not to be outdone, McGargel and Stan-
field gave their boots to a shoe store, which displayed the
muddy and worn footware in a place of honor in the store
window.

The four men were bombarded by letters. Most of them
offered simple congratulations. But one McGargel remembered in particular. With large letters in bright scarlet, it commented: "It must be great to be crazy and ride around in an
automobile." When they read this letter, the men laughed up-
roariously. Crazy? Yes, perhaps, they were crazy to spend a
month and a half being buffeted by rugged weather and
rocky roads, when sane persons could cross the country by

rail in seven days or less. But cars had something passenger trains lacked—an individuality, a freedom of movement, a joy of adventure. Whatever it was, the drivers agreed that horseless carriages had an immense appeal. Wouldn't it be strange if someday the whole country was crazy—crazy for cars!

7

Henry's Odd Contraptions

William Ford stared moodily across the farm fields. What, he pondered, should he do with a son like Henry? His school work had been poor and his spelling had been so bad that Henry himself sometimes could not understand what he had written. The teachers in the little country school Henry reluctantly attended had spent nearly as much time disciplining the mischievous youngster as they had trying to stuff *McGuffey's Reader* into his resisting brain. Henry practically had had a reserved dunce stool in front of the class. Even when Henry had not been trying to be bad, he had managed to create more than his share of disasters, like the time he burned down the school fence conducting an experiment with a coal-fired steam engine.

The elder Ford dug his hands into his pockets as he thought about his strange son. It wasn't that Henry was dumb. Far from it. He had a knack for things mechanical. Why, it had been almost senseless to give Henry toys when he was young, for he had taken them all apart within hours. Even such an expensive and complicated item as a watch would not remain in one piece once Henry got his fingers on it. At the age of thirteen Henry had managed not only to take his own watch apart but to reassemble it again in working order. When he was fifteen, Henry had crammed a workbench into his cramped bedroom to use in repairing timepieces for half the neighbors. It had gotten so that folks around joked that their clocks shuddered when Henry walked by.

Farmer Ford saw the wind ruffle the trees on some of his uncleared acreage. This was good land, he mused. Henry could have made a comfortable living here. But instead he had run off when he was just sixteen to work in Detroit machine shops. William Ford was surprised that his son's excitement with machinery hadn't cooled after being fired in just six days from his first job. Then he had lasted only nine months with a shop making fire hydrants. William chuckled. Henry had made $2.50 a week with that company, so little that he was losing money, for his room and board cost $3.50 a week.

Henry did a little better with his next job, making steam engines for the Detroit Drydock Co. Then he had spent a year traveling about the Midwest demonstrating farm machines for Westinghouse Engines. It was a footloose job that William Ford believed had no future.

If Henry's restless desire to change jobs constantly bothered William Ford, he also worried about Henry's health. As a youth, he had been thin as a wheat stalk. Even as a young man he was slight. He would never be robust, for when he was engaged in one of his endless mechanical projects, he would often forget to eat. If only Henry's mother had not died when he was thirteen. She might have been able to talk some sense of care for himself into the willful lad.

Yet William Ford had to admit that Henry was bright and quick-witted with mechanical, rather than intellectual, matters. And for all his half-pint size, he was a handsome youth. Girls liked him, perhaps because his boyish enthusiasm appealed to their motherly instincts. For whatever reason, William had not been surprised when Henry had married a spritely girl named Clara Bryant not long after she had hopped on one of his demonstration steam tractors and ridden merrily across the fields with him.

Farmer Ford smiled sadly. He had thought that after Clara became Henry's wife in 1888 he would settle down on the farm that William had given him. But Henry had stayed only until he had cut down most of the timber with a steam engine and sold the wood for profit. Now he was leaving again. William could see that Henry had machines in his bones. He was doomed to spend the rest of his life as a greasy mechanic.

Young Henry did not share his father's pessimism concerning his chosen career. His mind burned with excitement whenever he thought about machines—which was most of the time. As early as 1891 he believed he could build one of those newfangled gas engines small enough to fit on wheels and drive a buggy. When Clara asked him more about this engine, Henry carelessly yanked out a sheet of her favorite organ music and sketched an engine on the back.

The sketch showed how an engine could be made. Now all Henry had to do was to construct one. The Fords left the farm that same year and Henry went to work with the Edison Illuminating Company, which furnished electric light for most residences in Detroit. The hours were long, but Henry made time to work on his gasoline engine. First he fitted a homemade piston into an inch wide and foot long gas pipe, which was his cylinder. Then he fastened the piston by means

of a rod to a tiny crankshaft. After that he attached a flywheel from an old lathe onto the crankshaft. A gear on the
crankshaft operated a cam which opened intake and exhaust
valves at the top of the cylinder. The same gear timed an
electrical spark, which came from a couple of wires attached
to the kitchen outlet.

On Christmas Eve, 1893, thirty-year-old Henry set his
miniature engine up on the kitchen sink. With Clara carefully
dripping gasoline onto a screw which led to the intake valve,
Henry spun the flywheel. As the piston descended, the cam
opened the intake valve and gasoline was sucked into the
cylinder. When the piston rose to the cylinder top, a spark
exploded the gasoline vapor, hurling the piston downward.
Once down, the piston was forced upward by the spinning
flywheel on the crankshaft. The same motion caused the cam
to open the exhaust valve. The still-burning gasoline flamed
out. Then, as the piston sunk once more, the exhaust valve
closed and the intake valve opened. The gasoline was sucked
into the cylinder. When the piston rose once more, a spark
ignited the gas, and the process was repeated automatically.
Soon the kitchen was shaking with the engine's vibration and
the violent sputter of exploding gas.

Henry and Clara were awestruck at the little rumbling engine. It was as if they had created an entirely new species of
life. It lived on gasoline, spouted fire, and roared like a baby
tiger. It had its own smell, too. Henry and Clara coughed as
carbon monoxide began to sour the air. Henry switched off
the engine. The bedlam subsided; the piston rod moved ever
slower, then stopped. The little thing breathed fire no more.
It slumbered quietly. Yet there lay within it the potential for
renewed ferocity.

The young couple had given themselves a Christmas present which would not only change their lives, but would alter

the lives of their friends, relatives, and nearly every man, woman, and child in the entire nation.

But it was one thing to run a toy engine in the kitchen sink and quite another to construct a full-sized engine capable of driving a wheeled vehicle. Henry began gathering parts, not only for his big engine, but for the carriage which it would drive. Soon his collection included an assortment of bicycle tires, used carriage parts, and a couple of exhaust pipes from a discarded steam engine. Trying to form these and other items into a car was a long, tedious job. Henry could work only at night, for he had to keep his job with the electric company in order to scrape together funds with which to purchase his parts, to say nothing of supporting Clara. Henry's workshop was a cramped half shed behind the low-income dwelling on Bagley Street which he shared with another couple.

Slowly the auto began to emerge from the debris scattered about the shed. Ford had no idea just what the car's eventual size would be, and soon the frame began to push against the brick wall which divided Ford's half of the shed from the Bagley house's other tenant. After Ford talked his neighbor into storing his firewood in his kitchen, Ford knocked down the partition. When the bricks and dust had settled, Ford and Jim Bishop, who was helping him, resumed their night work.

By early June, 1896, the quadricycle, as Ford called his awkward-appearing invention, was ready for its first road test. Now Ford encountered another miscalculation. Before he could shove the thing from the shed, he had to whack out a row of bricks around the door. This was done without the knowledge of the owner of the house, but Ford hoped the man would not let a few bricks stand in the way of progress.

The great moment came. Ford and Bishop pushed the quadricycle into the wet darkness at 4 A.M., with sleepy-eyed Clara waiting for them under an umbrella.

Henry Ford in front of his Bagley Ave. garage. (FORD MOTOR CO.)

Ford spun the flywheel. He heard the motor suck in gasoline. Then the engine caught. Ford leaped to the seat and put the quadricycle into low gear (there were only two speeds and no reverse). The vehicle moved slowly forward. With Bishop riding ahead on a bike to warn whatever horse-drawn buggies were out at that hour, Ford bumped down the cobblestone alley. He drove very carefully, for the auto had no brakes. When he came to the street, he turned the steering lever (there was no steering wheel) and clattered down the dark, deserted avenue.

Although it was a drab early morning, Ford must have been wildly happy. He was moving under his own power. He could feel the two-cylinder engine sending surges of energy to the large flywheel that whirled rather close to the cushion upon which he was seated. As the flywheel whirred rapidly, making the little buggy vibrate like a tin can on a mountain slope, it turned a belt which was connected to a transmission wheel. Ford gingerly shoved his transmission lever forward from low to high gear. The belt shifted its position on the wheel and the vehicle moved faster.

Now misty rain slapped gently against Ford's face. Henry squinted into the darkness where Jim Bishop peddled along in front of him. Then Ford smiled to himself. Without Bishop what would a horse-traveler think when this strange apparition appeared before him—flames spurting from underneath while it moved without a horse or animal of any sort to propel it.

Suddenly, in the midst of Henry's joyous reveries, the auto stopped. When Ford and Bishop poked around the engine (which sat out in the open), they found that a piece from one of the sparking devices had broken. Leaving the car in front of the Cadillac Hotel, they went to a nearby Edison plant where Henry was known. By the time they had hunted up a replacement, a small crowd of hotel guests was goggling around the quadricycle. According to an eyewitness, the people found nothing to marvel at; instead, they could only wonder "who was crazy enough to spend a lot of time and money on such a contraption."

Ford got his machine started and left the hotel people smirking among themselves. Clara had a hot breakfast waiting for them when they returned home. When Ford got to work that morning, he didn't talk much about his accomplishment, for he knew the machine would be thought of as more a curiosity than anything to be proud of. Nor did he mind that his road test did not even make the Detroit newspapers. Rather, his first concern was to repair the whacked-out shed before the owner found out. He had hardly begun replacing the bricks, however, when the owner appeared. He exploded when he saw the damage. But even greater than his anger was his bewilderment as to why Ford had mutilated his shed. When Ford told him that he had taken his car out for a drive, the landlord forgot his anger in astonishment. "You mean the thing actually ran," he gasped. He told Ford to forget about adding bricks and to construct instead a swinging door so that he could get the auto in and out with ease.

The successful road test gave Ford enough confidence to take his quadricycle out in daylight. Soon Ford and his car became pests on the streets, as he revealed in his autobiography, *My Life and Work:*

> My "gasoline buggy" was the first and for a long time the only automobile in Detroit. It was considered to be something of a nuisance, for it made a racket and it scared horses. Also it blocked traffic. For if I stopped my machine anywhere in town a crowd was around it before I could start up again. If I left it alone even for a minute some inquisitive person always tried to run it. Finally, I had to carry a chain and chain it to a lamp post whenever I left it anywhere.
>
> And then there was trouble with the police. I do not know quite why, for my impression is that there were no speed-limit laws in those days. Anyway, I had to get a special permit from the mayor and thus for a time enjoyed the distinction of being the only licensed driver in America.

In the beginning, Ford did not dare to take his motorized buggy beyond the relatively smooth city streets. But after the thing proved it could run for an extended period of time without falling apart, he started on adventuresome rides into the country, taking a brave Clara and their little son, Edsel, with him. In a way the Ford family were like swimmers going out into a deep dangerous lake, for should the little quadricycle break down, they would be completely stranded with no place to go for parts. But Ford's drives were successful, and one day he mustered up all his courage and headed to his father's farm at Dearborn—a dozen miles from Detroit.

On this trip Henry was accompanied by Charlie King. King had been a referee at the Chicago race the year before and had undoubtedly given Ford many ideas which he incorporated into his quadricycle. Henry hoped King could back him up as to the quadricycle's future before his doubting father.

> Henry was as proud as could be [King remembered] when we swung through the farm gates. His father was a serious old fellow, a deacon and a justice of the peace and so on, and he came out of the house and just stood and stared at us. Some of the neighbors came by and stared too. I could see that old Mr. Ford was ashamed of a grown-up man like Henry fussing over a little thing like a quadricycle. We'd gone and humiliated him in front of his friends. Henry stood it as long as he could, then he turned to me and said, in a heartbroken way, "Come on, Charlie, let's you and me get out of here."

William Ford and his farm friends were not the only ones who thought Henry was rattlebrained for wasting his time on such a useless piece of machinery. Pedestrians shook their heads when Ford and his horseless carriage passed in a flurry of dust and exhaust fumes. Henry was aware of their disapproval and once, half in anger and half in good-natured play, he chased a man down the street in his quadricycle, clanging his gong at him as he fled in terror.

The car always attracted a swarm of hooting bicyclists—

sometimes two dozen or more. Ford could usually outdis-
tance them, and one time, when a large group approached
just after he had put his car in his garage, he gleefully directed them on a wild goose chase after they asked him where
the crazy horseless carriage had gone.

Although Ford had a big funny bone, as well as a knack
for practical jokes, he was devoted to a serious goal. He felt
certain that an improved gasoline carriage could eventually
provide inexpensive, rapid, and reliable transportation to the
masses of people who currently used horse buggies. But not
many persons at this early date shared Ford's conviction.
"Practically no one had the remotest notion of the future of
the internal combustion engine," he lamented. "There was no
demand for automobiles . . . the horseless carriage was considered merely a freak notion."

Despite the scoffers, Henry was convinced that gasoline
vehicles would play an important role in future transportation. Therefore, he quit his job with Edison Electric in 1899
to devote full time to making cars for the market. He was
able to sweet-talk a dozen or so men into investing fifteen
thousand dollars in the manufacture of his quadricycle. But
the company folded a year later. It had managed to throw
together only twenty autos, none of which aroused much
enthusiasm from the horse-loving public at large.

In November 1901, Ford tried again. He somehow convinced a few skeptical men to put up $30,500—a pitifully
small figure considering that Olds had needed $500,000 to
reach efficient production. To add further to Ford's problems, the company directors brought in feisty Henry Leland,
whose precision machine shop had done much work for Olds.

Leland was a cautious, inward-turned man with a thick
white beard and the drooping eyes of a beagle. He was
twenty years older than Ford. Ford was outgoing and any-

thing but cautious, and he took an immediate dislike to Leland. Leland, on his part, was aghast at Ford's unprofessional methods. Ford could not even read blueprints, and his method of inventing parts for a new motor was to have a pattern-maker whittle out a model in wood. If the model was not right, a second, third, or fourth was fashioned. This trial-and-error procedure wasted time and was primitive, Leland stated.

Within six months Ford resigned in disgust. The company then fell to Leland, who renamed it Cadillac, after the French founder of Detroit. Leland took the model that Ford had been working on, gave it a new engine manufactured in his ma-chine shop, and put it on the market. Within a few years Cadillac would join Oldsmobile as one of the nation's big two producers. But it was Ford who actually gave the company its start. Had he not resigned, there would have been no Cadillac.

Out of work again, Ford felt that before he could form yet a third company, he must bring his name to the public attention as that of a man able to construct a first-rate auto.

With this in mind, Henry, aided by Harold Wills and Tom Copper, began work on a racing car intended to be faster and more powerful than any the world had known. The weather was cold as the men worked in their unheated machine shop. When the temperature got so low that their fingers could not hold their tools (which had been loaned them by the shop owner), they donned boxing gloves and batted one another until they were warm. After six weary months the monster machine was completed. Ford named it the 999, after an ex-press locomotive that sped between New York and Chicago.

The 999 boasted four large cylinders delivering an almost unheard of 80 horsepower. When the engine started, the roar was so loud that Ford claimed it was enough "to half kill a man." To drive the great machine over a racetrack roughened by countless horses hooves was a rugged experience. "Going over Niagara Falls would have been a pastime," Ford commented, compared with a ride in the 999. Ford put only a single seat in the racer, for "one life to a car was enough."

As Ford began taking the 999 on trial runs, he found that the car presented certain problems. For one, Ford, being slight of build, had a difficult time controlling 999 with the "T" shaped bar that served in place of a steering wheel. To turn the 999, Ford had to place a hand on the knobs at each end of the bar, then shove the bar one direction or the other. It required great skill, as well as a lion's strength to keep the car on course.

The difficulty of steering was greatly intensified by the car's tendency to send a drenching spray of engine oil over Ford as he drove. This oil coated his goggles, making it almost impossible to see anything of the racetrack except a murky blur. Ford's appearance after driving the 999 was humorous to reporters covering the race preparations. One reporter wrote that he found Ford to be "a daub of oil from head to foot," and Ford's tie "looked as though it had been cooked in lard."

Although Ford had a daredevil streak, he knew that the 999 was more than he could handle. Frantically he began searching for someone strong enough and insane enough to drive the oil-splattering racer. It wasn't until a week before the big event, scheduled for October 25, 1902, that Ford came up with the adventuresome athlete he needed. This was the soon-to-be-famous Barney Oldfield: he of steel-blue eyes, a boxer's square jaw, and such a scoffing attitude toward death that just before the race he joked with Ford: "This chariot may kill me, but they will say afterward that I was going like hell."

Henry Ford and Barney Oldfield, 1902. (FORD MOTOR CO.)

Barney pitted the 999 against the Bullet of prominent car maker and ace driver, Alex Winton, along with two other crack racers. The race was held before an excited crowd on a five-mile track just outside Detroit. The cars were cranked up. Flames spouted from their exhausts. The air vibrated to the thunder of their engines. The starting flag went down and they were off!

Oldfield roared into the lead. He took the curves with an open throttle. The 999 teetered and skidded, but Oldfield managed to hold it on the track. Oil spurted over him, obscuring his vision. Still he kept the 999 at full speed. Winton was on his tail as the two pulled away from the other cars. By the second mile it was Oldfield and Winton, with the 999 grinding out a slim lead. By the third mile the 999 began pulling away from the Bullet. As they started the fourth mile circuit, Winton developed motor trouble. Reluctantly, he pulled out of the race.

But Oldfield kept up his ferocious pace. Soon he lapped the rear car. Then, tearing to the finish line, he also lapped the third car. As he streaked across, the timekeepers gasped. Five miles in only a few seconds over five minutes! That was close to 60 miles an hour—the legendary mile-a-minute! It was an American record that would stand until one of Ransom Old's souped-up cars shaded it out a year later.

People everywhere were impressed with Ford's engineering of the 999, for it had been less than seven years since the Duryeas had won the Chicago race with a car that staggered along at barely 8 mph.

Now Ford was ready for his third venture into automobile manufacturing. He knew he must not fail this time or he might never be able to attract backers again!

8

The Magic Company

Alexander Malcomson was a tall, husky man with frizzy side whiskers and a floor-brush mustache. Because he was willing to work like a mule and take chances like a fox, he had rapidly built up a fine coal business that not only supplied most of Detroit's households with fuel, but also supplied railroads, steamships, and factories. Most persons in eastern Michigan and western Ohio were familiar with Malcomson's freight wagons boasting his clever slogan, "Hotter Than Sunshine."

As a nodding friend and fellow churchgoer of Henry Ford, Malcomson had heard enthusiastic descriptions of the future of automobiles. At first the coal tycoon had tended to chuckle inwardly, for many persons thought that Henry, with his one-sided mania for horseless buggies, was a little nutty. And Malcomson knew that Henry had already failed with two prior companies. Yet Malcomson also knew that Henry had occupied a position of responsibility with the

well-managed Edison Company before he had quit several
years back to devote himself to auto development. Malcomson was also impressed with Ford's earnestness and his con-
tagious enthusiasm. It was Ford's enthusiasm more than anything else that convinced Malcomson to give him cautious
backing in the initial phase of his third company.

Thus, in August 1902, Malcomson invested five hundred
dollars in Ford. It was an almost microscopic amount with
which to begin an auto enterprise, but it was the best Henry
could do, what with a pair of failures behind him. To celebrate the partnership, both Malcomson and Ford shaved off
their mustaches. Then Malcomson went back to his coal
business and Ford was left to construct a demonstration car.

Ford began with just one man, Harold Wills, his skilled
assistant from the 999. Soon they were joined by Jim Couzens,
a sharp-witted office manager on loan from Malcomson.
While Ford and Wills laid out plans for the car, Couzens
tended to the purchasing of tools and car parts, the hiring
of a dozen workmen, and all the numerous nonengineering
duties for which Ford had neither the interest nor the apti-
tude.

Success seemed a long way off to the humble trio who
now began laying the foundation for what would become,
in the not too distant future, America's greatest automotive
empire. They rented a little wood-frame building on Mack
Avenue that had formerly been used as a carpenter shop. It
was a crude, junky place. In it Ford dumped a couple of
drills, a grinding wheel, and an ancient forge that cast an
unearthly glow and a hellish heat. Henry, in overalls and with
grease on his face, was more like one of the workmen than
the boss. He called the men by their first names and they
called him "Hank."

Ford always had a good word to give his crew. Soon

they learned to watch for the mischievous twinkle in his eyes that warned them that he was planning one of his practical jokes. Ford's tricks kept the dozen workers in a happy humor that contrasted with their drab, cluttered surroundings. There was the trick Ford pulled when he nailed one man's hat to the floor. As the poor fellow tugged at his hat, the rest of the men roared with laughter. And the old nail trick worked again when a chap changed to his work shoes, then found he couldn't walk because the soles had been fastened to the floor.

One never knew what would happen when he grasped a door handle, for Ford often fixed up a weak electric current on the other end. Yet the men liked their odd employer, and, as the company grew in later years, most of the men at the little Mack Avenue plant rose to occupy positions of responsibility and high pay.

But during the hectic days of 1902, few dreamed of what lay in the future, for the company was barely avoiding bankruptcy. Ford and his workers were in a race with time, since the demonstration car had to be ready before Malcomson's meager investment ran out.

By Thanksgiving the engine was completed. Wills rummaged about his attic to form the FORD insignia out of some old print he had used when he was a boy of fifteen. Soon the chassis was hammered together. Then the jazzy little car was given a steering wheel—an ultramodern innovation for those used to the usual lever to turn the wheels.

Once the car was put together, Jim Couzens trudged about Detroit's financial areas trying to talk some of the wealthy citizens into investing in Ford stock. It was a heartbreaking time for the man who would one day not only be a United States senator but a millionaire in his own right. One businessman ushered Couzens out of his office so brusquely that he sat on the street curb fighting tears. Couzens' work was made ever more difficult when Wills wrecked the pilot car while taking it on a test run down Mack Avenue. With their cash now almost gone, and no demonstration car to show investors, Ford and his crew began frantic work on a second car.

The second car was hardly completed before Ford made a bold decision. Even though he was aware that he was virtually broke—as well as the fact that few investors had yet indicated any interest in his company—Ford decided to go ahead with plans to produce cars in quantity for the spring 1903 market.

Accordingly, Ford contracted the Dodge brothers, who owned one of Detroit's best machine shops. He asked the Dodges to furnish him with 650 car frames. The order totled $162,500, which Ford assured the Dodges he would pay when the frames arrived. It was a wild thing to do, since Ford had no money of his own, Malcomson would certainly not meet such a huge bill, and Ford company stock was a laughable commodity among Detroit's haughty financial bigwigs.

The Dodges were not stupid men. They knew they would be left with a warehouse full of unusable frames if Ford was unable to meet their bill. And, more than that: the Dodges would have to invest sixty thousand dollars of their own money for special equipment to make the frames according to Ford's specifications. Furthermore, the Dodges already had a profitable contract to make frames for Oldsmobile, which they would have to give up if they concentrated on Ford.

The brothers, John and Horace, were quick-tempered redheads. They were quarrelsome and pugnacious and got along with few persons. At this moment of their lives, the Dodges were discontented with the Olds contract. Knowing Ford's dependence on them, they negotiated a hard-nosed agreement with him that would eventually make them rich men and enable them to begin a motor company of their own. Thus it might be said that the Dodges enabled Ford cars to be produced and Ford later enabled Dodge cars to be produced.

The Dodges' contract called for the two brothers to receive a full 10 percent of Ford's stock in addition to the profit they would make from the sale of the 650 car frames. For this 10 percent (which within a few years would be worth millions) the Dodges would pay nothing until Ford reimbursed them for the frames. Then they would use part of the profits to purchase the stock. Thus, in a way, Ford himself would be paying for the Dodges' stock in his own company.

Yet it was not quite as rosy an agreement was pictured, for the problem still remained of where Ford would get the money to pay for the frames. And, if he had not gotten it, both the Ford and the Dodge Motor companies would never have been heard of.

The knotty problem began unraveling as Ford began to assemble autos in his Mack Avenue plant. When news reached the public that the famous racer, Henry Ford, was actually making a car for sale, inquiries about the Model A (as Ford called it) began trickling into Detroit. Although Ford still had no car for the market, these inquiries indicated a demand for Ford cars. Malcomson and Couzens were now able to sell enough stock to provide twenty-eight thousand dollars in cash to keep the company afloat.

Once a few stockholders had been rounded up, the Ford-Malcomson partnership was dissolved and a corporation was formed in its place. The formal beginning of the company

Henry Ford driving his 1903 Model A. (FORD MOTOR CO.)

occurred at a meeting on the evening of June 13, 1903. The tiny company had been able to attract only seven investors besides Ford, Malcomson, Couzens, and the two Dodges. Since Alexander Malcomson owned as much stock as Ford (between them they had 51 percent), the corporation should have been called Malcomson-Ford Motors. But the coal tycoon, probably smirking at his craftiness, evidently decided he would rather not have his good name associated with such a risky venture as auto making. Therefore the new corporation was called simply the Ford Motor Company. Malcomson's man, John Gray, was voted president and Henry Ford, who had invested his time but no money, had to be content with the vice–presidency.

The company was hardly begun before it was in financial quicksand. Of the twenty-eight thousand dollars originally invested, five thousand dollars had been paid to the Dodges for part of their frame order. Another ten thousand dollars had gone to reimburse Malcomson for the money he had paid to the Dodges as part of the old Ford-Malcomson partnership. When these payments were combined with other bills, the struggling company had almost no cash left.

Despite visions of his other two failures, and ignoring the disquieting fact that he had as yet no firm orders to purchase any of his cars, Ford went bravely ahead with his production.

Stockholders held their breath as the bank balance dipped. One day it stood at a bare $224! At that moment almost any bill could have broken the company. Certainly a swarm of doubts and misgivings must have stung the investors, who wondered why they had been so stupid as to give money to an eccentric mechanic like Henry Ford. How could they have hoped to compete with popular, well-established cars like the Columbia, the Winton, or the Haynes-Apperson!

Actually the investors had a right to tremble. The entire auto industry had a rather disreputable reputation. Most of the cars made were shoddy, more like movable junk heaps than reliable transportation vehicles. Gas tanks would leak and drive chains would snap; tires would shred easily. Occasionally, entire motors would drop onto the roadbed where they would lie hissing and gurgling. When a driver would try

to purchase repair parts for his dying auto, he would often
be told that the company had not gotten around to manufacturing them.

This led to the most frightening terror for those who
had invested in Ford's faltering future. This was the fact that,
as yet, the vast majority of people had not the slightest intention of buying one of those horseless-carriage contraptions.
They thought of cars as strictly toys for the rich. One reason
for this was that most cars simply cost too much—around
$2,500 in 1903 ($15,000 at modern prices). Considering that
one could purchase a spanking new buggy and a prancing
horse for $500, it seemed obvious that there would never be a
mass market for autos.

Then, too, since there were few trained mechanics, one
had to hire a chauffeur to drive the car and to lie on his
back in the middle of a dirt road to repair it when it broke
down.

Furthermore, the auto-things were next to useless during
the cold or rainy months, for they had no metal tops. In bad
weather one had to put up a frame roof, button down a flimsy
leather top, and hang opaque curtains from the sides. The
rain and cold would rush through the gaps, leaving riders
so miserable that few cared to take out a car from November
to the end of April.

Large numbers of persons bore an outright hostility
toward the horseless carriages, with their antagonizing noise,
stinking exhaust fumes, and representation of wealthy snob-
bery. Writer Booth Tarkington, who grew up in the era,
described these early cars and the feeling toward them in
The Magnificent Ambersons:

> Like a cowboy shooting up a peaceful camp, a frantic devil-
> auto would hurtle out of a distance, bellowing exhaust,

racketing like a machine gun gone amuck—and at these horrid sounds the surreys and buggies would hug the curbstone, and the bicyclists scatter to cover, cursing; while children would rush from the sidewalks to drag pet dogs from the street. The thing would roar by, leaving a long wake of turbulence; then the indignant street would quiet down for a few minutes—till another auto came.

Isabel Amberson, the story's heroine, saw the horseless carriages as nuisances that must be abolished:

> I've begun to agree with George about cars being more a fad than anything else, and I think it must be the height of the fad just now. You know how roller-skating came in . . . and now only a few children use rollers for getting to school. Besides, people won't permit the automobiles to be used. Really, I think they'll make laws against them. You see how they spoil the bicycling and the horse driving; people just seem to hate them! They'll never stand it—never in the world! . . . I shouldn't be really surprised to see a law passed forbidding the sale of automobiles, just the way there is with concealed weapons.

Even for those daring sports who enjoyed automobiling, it was an awful lot of work preparing oneself for a drive. Since cars always kicked up dense clouds of dust when it was dry or sheets of mud when it was wet, both men and women had to don long, awkward fitting coats called, with good reason, dusters. In addition, the men, who usually drove, slapped wide-rimmed goggles over their eyes and put heavy gloves over their hands. The women covered their hair with huge hats. To protect their eyes thick veils hung down from the hats. So completely did the protective clothing cover the riders that the only way friends could tell who they were was by first recognizing the car.

Once clothed and in the car, there was a frustrating lack

of places to go. The United States at this time had only one hundred fifty thousand miles of surfaced roads, compared with more than two hundred twenty thousand miles of railroad lines. Not only was it far easier to get places by rail, but the so-called surfaced roads were merely rough byways of rutted, bump-strewn gravel. Such roads were satisfactory for slow-moving, horse-drawn buggies or wagons. But these roads would leave a motorist roaring along at 20 mph shaken from his goggles to his garters.

Should an auto enthusiast desire to drive to a town more than a few miles distant, he had to load his car with an expensive array of implements. He needed a five-gallon gasoline can, for gas stations were as far apart as oases in a desert. Then he required a funnel and a chamois-skin strainer to rid the gas of impurities which would clog the engine. He had to carry a large toolbox with a jack, wrenches, and tire patches, since he could expect an endless series of blowouts to enliven every inter-town expedition. He had to have a tin bucket, which was essential when he needed to fill the ever-steaming radiator with creek water. And, of course, he needed the tools vital to free the auto when it ran off the road or became stuck in the midst of a muddy stream. These tools included a block and tackle for the tough jobs, as well as a shovel to dig out obstructions and an axe to make lever poles to push the car through mudholes.

William Faulkner, in *The Reivers*, gives a vivid account of what travelers encountering a swampy creek bottom around 1903 could expect:

> . . . the automobile lurched, canted, and hung [commented the story's hero, Lucius, almost twelve years old] . . . Boon was already removing his shoes and socks and rolling up his pants. "All right," he said to Ned over his shoulder, "get out."

"I got my Sunday clothes on," Ned said.

"So have I," Boon said. . . .

| While Lucius seated himself at the steering wheel, the two men sloshed through the mud. Boon chopped two sapling trees. | "Take a-holt of this pole," [he said to Ned] . . . "All right"—to me—"ease her ahead now and whenever she bites, keep her going." Which we did, Boon and Ned levering their poles forward under the back axle, pinching us forward for another lurch of two or three or sometimes five feet, until the car hung spinning again, the whirling back wheels coating them both with mud from knee to crown. . . .

Although Lucius and his companions worked until they were exhausted, they could not get their car out of Hell Creek and were forced to pay a farmer with a mule team to haul them through the ever-worsening muck.

Sometimes experiences such as Hell Creek were not even the most frustrating of a day's travel. It was not unusual for a tourist to bump along for hours without knowing where he was, for there were no numbered highways, no accurate road maps, and few gas stations with reliable road information. One had to depend on homemade signs stuck to trees or fence posts to indicate the direction of the next town. And when one asked directions from a native, he would likely get an answer like: "Well, I reckon if you go couple or so miles in the direction you're headed you'll see a barn with the door off its hinge—unless it's been fixed. To get to Centerville, turn right for a spell, then make a sharp left. After you ford two creeks, watch for a grove of maples. Cut through the maples on the farmer's road. Keep to the right fork. At the fallen elm, veer off to your left; and after a while you'll see Centerville. Unless you miss it."

Such directions as these sent tourists blindly across the

countryside. Sometimes a driver and his family would spend an entire day searching for a nearby town.

This was the world into which Henry Ford was determined to sell his car. The wonder was not that he had a difficult time attracting investors but that anyone at all would be so foolish as to put money into such a perilous enterprise.

Ford's Model A, while not a great car even by 1903 standards, was good enough to impress certain adventurous businessmen. These men wished to be Ford dealers and their requests came to Couzens, who handled that end of the enterprise. Couzens shipped the first cars off to his new dealers. These dealer purchases brought a net profit to the company of nearly forty thousand dollars for the first three-and-a-half-months operation. This was twelve thousand dollars more than the original investment and enabled the company to declare a 10 percent dividend on November 21. It was an encouraging beginning.

The Model A sold for $850—or $50 more if one wanted a sporty rear seat (called a tonneau) placed over the engine. To help his dealers sell the Model A, Ford's advertising described it in glowing terms that bore little relationship to rocky reality. He called his little roadster "perfect," and claimed it would "provide a luxurious means of travel"[!] He proclaimed that it would "carry you 'jarlessly' over any kind of half–decent roads." And to cap it all, his ads pictured a dreamy sort of Model A motoring experience where "you can—if you choose—loiter lingeringly through shady avenues or you can press down on the foot-lever until all the scenery looks alike to you and you have to keep your eyes skinned to count the milestones as they pass."

Of course, people knew the ads were mostly hoopla, for there was no vehicle anywhere that could take a person over

America's hashed-up roads "jarlessly." Yet the Fordmobile (as the Model A was first called in imitation of the Oldsmobile) was as good a car as most, and cheaper than almost all. Ford's first year's sales were 1,700 cars, which was excellent, though not in the class with the pacesetters: Oldsmobile with 5,000 and Cadillac with 3,000.

The following year was disappointing, however. Malcomson demanded that the company get into the large-car market. Since he owned as much stock as Ford himself, Henry had to oblige. Reluctantly, Ford designed Model B, a four-cylinder car based on his massive 999 racer. It sold for $2,000. Meanwhile, Ford put out two smaller cars: the Model C and Model F, which were two-cylinder vehicles much like his discontinued Model A. However, the two cars sold for more than the good old A: C went for around $900 and F for $1,000.

Ford felt that there was no better way to promote the Model B than to set a speed record with the Arrow racer, twin of the 999 and the prototype upon which Model B was based. For this purpose, Ford had a long segment of snow cleared from the ice on Michigan's Lake St. Clair. Cinders were then scattered over the ice. On January 9, 1904, Ford and a companion made ready to challenge the world speed record. Clara Ford, with their ten-year-old son, Edsel, watched nervously in the cold. Other spectators too clustered about the track, most coming from the nearby Hotel Chesterfield. The crowd hummed with excitement, for it was not everyday that one could see a local fellow try to set a world record, especially over such a dangerous track. Anything could happen.

> I shall never forget that race [Ford recalled]. The ice seemed smooth enough, so smooth that if I had called off

the trial we should have secured an immense amount of the wrong kind of advertising. But instead of being smooth, that ice was seamed with fissures which I knew were going to mean trouble the moment I got up speed. But there was nothing to do but go through with the trial, and I let the old "Arrow" out. At every fissure the car leaped into the air. I never knew how it was coming down. When I wasn't in the air, I was skidding, but somehow I stayed top side up and on the course, making a record that went all over the world!

Ford had whizzed over the ice at more than 90 mph. Later he held a victory dinner at Hotel Chesterfield, where he and his elated companions feasted on roasted muskrat.

Although Ford could boast that his racing feat "put Model B on the map," it was not enough to make large numbers of buyers want the big, expensive auto. During the year 1904–1905, the company sold only 45 more cars than in its first year. And in 1905–1906 sales actually went down to 1,599 cars! Ford Motors was on the skids.

The result was a tooth and claw battle for control between Ford, who wanted to base the company's future on a cheap car for the masses, and Malcomson, who wanted a truly luxurious car even finer than Model B for the wealthy. Since both men held equal shares, neither could force the other out. After much wrangling, it was decided that the company should produce one luxury and one cheap car. Then the buyers would decide which would bring in the greater profit.

Model K was the fancy car. It sold for $2,800 (nearly $17,000 at modern prices), had six cylinders, and was represented to be precisely what a rich, sporting man would like to spin about in. The Model N, on the other hand, was a stripped-down auto selling for only $600.

The demand for Model N was instantaneous—for it was without question one of the finest cheap cars on the market. Among the N's main selling points was the fact that it had a four-cylinder engine which offered the driver a far smoother ride than the jerky two cylinders of the competitive cars. Even as the Ns began rolling out of Ford's new and larger factory on Piquette Avenue, company designers came out with better variations: Models R and S.

Alas, for Model K—its reception was quite different. The Vanderbilts and Rockefellers had dozens of makes to choose from, and Malcomson's entry was no better than those put out by Pope, Winton, Duryea, and Oldsmobile (whose officials had removed Ransom Olds when he had fought against dropping a more modern version of his single-cylinder Curved Dash.)

Ford management did everything it could to sell the Model K. The price was dropped by a full 20 percent. Dealers were not permitted to purchase Model N's unless they took a certain number of K's. But it did no good. By the middle of 1906 it was clear that K, for all its splashy good looks, was a weak brother to N. On July 12, Malcomson sold all his stock to Ford and left the company. Henry had won total victory.

With Malcomson out of the way, Ford was the majority stockholder. He could now do whatever he wished. And what he wished was to produce a car that would appeal to the little folk. This was a consuming desire with him. He did not care that scoffers reminded him that the rich lived in cities where paved streets were ideal for driving but the little folk lived predominantly in the country where roads were suitable for horses only. Nor did he believe the scoffers when they asked how farmers could get their cars repaired when there were no mechanics in the country. Where, too, would the farmers get gasoline, the doubters continued. And, most important of all, why should a farmer buy a car at all when old Dobbin, with a wagon attachment, cost only around five hundred dollars—far less than any car, even Model N. Nearly all experts agreed: the future of cars lay with the luxury, not the cheap, models.

But Henry could only answer with his half-shy, half-arrogant smile. He had grown up on a farm. He knew that there was a market there. Make the car, and the gas stations, mechanics, and even the roads would follow. Look at Model N. It had brought Ford sales up from 1,599 in 1905–1906 to 8,500 the following year. Certainly this proved there was a market. So he went ahead with his radical plans to concentrate on a cheap car.

In the two years that followed, Ford's faith in his car was dramatically proven right. As the yearly sales of models N, R, and S jumped to nearly eleven thousand, the profits of the Ford Company soared. In 1906, the company had paid a measly $10,000 in dividends; in 1907 the total was an astonishing $100,000. This, however, was just the beginning. In 1908, dividends reached $600,000. And the following year, dividends reached a boggling $1,800,000! Since Ford owned 58 percent of the stock, he received most of these dividend bonanzas. Within the brief span of three years he became so very rich that Clara once found a crumpled check for $75,000 that he had completely forgotten about in one of his pants pockets!

But it wasn't only Ford who reaped a fortune on the cheap little cars that hardly anyone had thought would sell. Jim Couzens had stripped his savings account, worked a moonlight job, and borrowed from a bank to scrape up the $2,400 he invested in Ford in 1903. In return, he received more than $300,000 in dividends plus a stock payment worth $200,000

—for a total of half-a-million dollars! The two Dodge brothers accumulated nearly that much between them, to say nothing of the vast profits they made from selling Ford a large percentage of his car parts. Even Couzens' sister, Rosetta, who taught school in Detroit, received an unbelievable shower of dividend dollars. At the insistence of her brother, she had reluctantly put a bare hundred dollars into the venture. By the time the dividends and stock payments had been totaled in 1909, Rosetta had made $50,000, which in modern times would equal $300,000.

How had it all happened? Ford himself said "the business went along almost as by magic." And certainly Ford had a great deal of luck at being ready with a workable auto at precisely the moment when the American buying public was first becoming accustomed to regarding a car as a necessity rather than merely an expensive novelty.

But there were dozens of other manufacturers competing with Ford—some as small as he, many far larger. When the magic of the moment was gone, the fact was that Ford possessed three assets over the others. First, his success at racing established him as a nationally known figure with a reputation for producing champion vehicles. Second, he was able to take his racing engine and adapt it to a light, cheap car. As Ford—who was never known for his modesty—later boasted: his cars "were tough, they were simple, and they were well made." The toughness and well-crafted manufacture enabled them to stand up to the grueling roads over which other cars failed. The engine simplicity meant that the ordinary driver, even if he was no mechanic, could repair the car should trouble develop far from a service station, which was almost always the case in these early days.

The third asset, which Ford habitually underestimated, was that he had Jim Couzens working for him. No car, however well made, could sell without a high-power sales force to reach the public through efficient car dealerships. The sales end was all Couzens'.

Clara had stood staunchly by Henry during the lean times when most people who knew him thought he'd never amount to a hill of bolts. Ford's own father had been one of these and had died without knowing otherwise. But Clara had always felt that Henry would be a success, and she had never complained at their modest homes or at the diverting of Henry's income into engines rather than into the small luxuries that her friends enjoyed.

As the huge sums of money began accumulating, Henry decided to build Clara a mansion to make up for the many things she had done without for so long. It was a huge, imposing house two-and-a-half stories high made of red brick with handsome stone trim. There was ample space for the team of servants who had their own dining room. Henry included a garage-workshop for his son, Edsel (who gave Henry a foretaste of his skill with machinery by cutting off the tip of a finger with a power tool).

Henry could have retired and lived in splendor. But, as a vigorous man of forty-six, he was in what he considered the prime of life. He loved the automotive world: the whir of gears, the clang of presses, the throb of gas engines. He wanted the active life, not the numbness of a rocking chair. He felt that he had a lot more to contribute to the fledgling auto industry. For even with the resounding success of models N, R, and S, Ford knew that eleven thousand car sales a year was a trifling number. In a country with more than 20 million families who needed a cheap and reliable means of transportation, Ford's current sales represented a percent too minute to be computed. Furthermore, Ford had to admit that his horseless carriages, as they now functioned, could probably never reach the masses. They were good, but not quite good enough. They broke down a little too often. They were not completely comfortable for a wife and children. They were somewhat too hard for the average, nonmechanical man to repair with ease. They were a little too expensive.

Ford decided to put his best experts to work on a new model—one which would be as near perfection as man could make. It would be cheap; it would sell for no more than a horse and buggy. He would make such a car, and it would reach that 20 million family market.

So, secretly, Henry Ford resumed his magic. He gathered a team of his top specialists together and put them in a walled-off room. There they began work on Ford's dream car.

It was called the Model T.

9

Queen Lizzie

Henry Ford walked through the nearly deserted third floor of his factory. In a far corner of the room he came to the sealed-off section where his experts were working behind a bolted door. Entering the room, Ford eased his slim body into a rocking chair. Crossing his legs and smiling, he began rocking slowly back and forth. Quickly the men were comfortable with their boss. Ford listened as ideas were tossed among them. Joe Galamb sketched each innovation on a blackboard. The specialists went over each sketch mercilessly, for all of them were eager to come up with a fine car.

After Ford had approved the suggestions, he would leave to attend to other business. Then the others would grind out the new part on one of the power machines in the secret room. When Ford returned later in the afternoon, he would often help with a wrench or drill as the part was fitted to the engine block or to the emerging car frame.

Sometimes Henry would do a lot more work. Such as the

time when they were having a great deal of trouble with the revolutionary new electronic device called a magneto. Henry labored forty-two hours without rest along with one of his experts, dipping the magneto in a special varnish bubbling in an old syrup kettle that Henry had brought from the Ford farm. But when they were through, the magneto worked and the stage was set for the later development of the modern generator.

It took the team four long years to perfect the Model T. But gradually the pace-setting car began to materialize in the cramped workshop. Excitement among the group was intense as the long-awaited day came when they opened the door and pushed their creation into the main plant.

Workmen dropped their tools to gasp at it. The car was truly impressive. With its size and spaciousness, it was difficult to believe that the car was designed to sell for under one thousand dollars. There were murmurs of awe as Ford took the Model T down to the street. When he cranked the engine up, it purred with the authority of its four well-built cylinders. George Holley took the steering wheel and Ford leaped into the seat beside him. As the crowd of workers cheered, Holley put the car into gear. It leaped forward and they were off on the Model T's first trial run.

Ford was as excited as a child. His face was one glorious smile as they bounced in noisy majesty down Detroit's main street. People stared at the two laughing men and their machine. Most Detroiters had grown used to cars by this time, and few realized that here was a creation that would change the face of America. But Ford and Holley knew, and they made a special detour to parade slowly past the office of Alexander Malcomson. Ford could not resist taunting his former partner with his masterpiece.

When Ford returned to Piquette Avenue, his workmen

were still there. The car worked beautifully, Ford announced, beaming. Everyone was bubbling with enthusiasm—Ford even more than the others. "Every time he'd meet some-body," remembered worker George Brown, "he'd give him a kick in the pants or a punch between the shoulders." Rais-ing his voice above the others, Ford shouted in triumph: "Well, I guess we've got it started!"

And indeed he had.

When news of the car reached the public, there was an in-stant stir. It wasn't only that the price was so low, for there were other cheap cars on the market. But Ford's Model T was really finely built. All four cylinders of the engine were cast at the same time, making the block much more sturdy than other cars, where the cylinders were cast sepa-rately then assembled into the motor. And Ford made free use of vanadium steel—the toughest steel yet perfected—in his crankshafts, springs, axles, and gears. Not even cars which were more expensive used vanadium, for it was Ford who had brought the innovation to America from Europe. Furthermore, the Model T was especially designed to ride high over the ruts that whanged apart the undersides of other cars traveling America's deeply rutted country roads. All in all the Model T stood a full seven feet high when the top was up.

The wonders of the amazing Model T did not stop here. The car was safer than most, with two braking systems: one working on the wheel drums and the other through the trans-mission. The transmission itself was a dream. The gears of other cars were difficult to shift, especially in the cold weather. The Model T, on the other hand, had a uniquely engineered planetary transmission, which was easy to operate and became the forerunner of modern gear arrangements.

With all its revolutionary advancements, the Model T was a symphony of simplicity. Nobody with the slightest mechanical ability would have difficulty making minor repairs. Even major problems could be handled by a village blacksmith. It was truly the people's car.

Even before the first Model T's began rolling off the Piquette production line, the public was almost frantic to buy them. In anticipating the demand for his tough, cheap car, Ford had mobilized his factory and his workmen as if for war. Yet he had never imagined that the wave of orders would so swamp him that by May 1, 1909, he would be able to accept no more orders until August! Nothing like this had ever happened before in the auto industry.

When Ford was again ready for orders, the flood continued. By 1910, sales had leaped from eleven thousand of the prior year to nineteen thousand. Astounding as this number seemed, in 1911 sales doubled! And they doubled again the following year, when they reached almost eighty thousand.

The nation was going happily insane over Ford's Tin Lizzies, as the Model T's were soon affectionately known. People everywhere were falling in love with them just as if they had been creatures alive. "Boys used to veer them off the highway into a level pasture [one oldtimer recalled] and run wild with them, as though they were cutting up with a girl."

Sales continued to soar. Soon Ford was making so much money that he was a millionaire many times over. In one single year alone, he received $16 million in dividends. Profits no longer meant anything to him. What he wanted was to bring his Model T to everyone—to actually replace the family horse with a Model T. His goal became to sell, sell, sell.

To take advantage of mass production, he built another new plant, this one the largest auto factory in America. It was located at Highland Park, Michigan, near the farm where his father had once written off his unusual son as a failure. With the production economies that the new plant with its revolutionary moving assembly line afforded, Ford found he could lower the Tin Lizzie's price even further. The car originally had sold for $850. Two years later, Ford had it down to $750. By 1915, it was $440, and in 1916 it hit the market at just $360.

To get this unheard of figure, Ford eliminated all frills—right down to the windshield wiper, which was operated by hand. Even in the matter of paint, Ford did not wish to slow

Ford Model T pickup truck, around 1919. (FORD MOTOR CO.)

his mass production line with various colors. "A customer can have a car painted any color he wants," Ford quipped, "so long as it is black." The public evidently agreed that a low price was more important than a snappy color. By 1916, the Model T sales had rocketed to six hundred thousand.

Soon there was hardly a street, avenue, or farmyard that did not have a gleaming Tin Lizzie proudly on display. For many plain folk, the sturdy boxlike car was the most thrilling purchase of their lives.

When Gramp Longstreet brought home his newly bought Tin Lizzie, young Stevie gasped in wonder at the black beauty. "When I first saw the car it shone with the splendor of what I supposed Roman high life must have glittered with," Stephen Longstreet recalled.

It wasn't long before Stevie was infected with the same wanderlust that was gnawing at Gramp and Sari, Stevie's young and beautiful mother. As soon as the snow had melted in the spring of 1919, the three of them climbed eagerly into their flivver and headed for high adventure on their way from New York City to California and back. As an adult Steve later recreated this vagabond journey in a book entitled *The Boy in the Model T*.

Gramp was well outfitted. Over the upper portion of his face he wore large goggles. In his pockets he had an assortment of wrenches, screwdrivers, pliers, and various lengths of wires, pins, steel nuts, and whatever else he thought he might need to repair the car on the long trip where mechanics would be in very short supply.

The flivver itself was stuffed with every conceivable item that the three daredevils might need. Dumped into the back seat were clothing bags which stuck up like chimneys (for the Model T had no trunk). Rising from the floorboards

were boxes of hams and bacon and canned fruits and vege-
tables. Wedged in between them were tins of coffee and sugar.
Lashed onto the running board (that foot-wide platform that
extended from the rear fender to the front fender) was a
folding steel camp stove and a small icebox. To balance off
the food gear, the other running board was stacked with
three large steel cans marked: Water, Gas, and Oil. These
were vital items, for service stations were nearly as scarce as
paved roads.

After the packing was done, Gramp helped Sari ascend
the mountain of gear and supplies in the back seat, where she
made herself a cubbyhole and wrapped a buffalo robe about
her. Then Stevie clambered into the car over the stove and
icebox on one running board and Gramp hoisted himself
over the gas, water, and oil cans on the other side.

Once in the driver's seat, Gramp clamped his teeth tightly
on his ever-present cigar and lowered his goggles. "We're
ready!" he shouted, triumphant that he had managed to pack
up without Lizzie splitting apart or bending an axle.

Stevie's father, who was staying home to run the family
business, took hold of the starting crank. Gramp turned on
the spark and adjusted the gas levers. Papa jerked the crank
with a circular motion, being ready to snatch his hand away
when the engine caught—for a backward kick of the crank
had broken more than one man's arm.

With a vicious roar, the motor started. Papa jumped
clear. Gramp gripped the steering wheel as if he were clutch-
ing a life preserver. He jammed Lizzie into low gear. With
a violent series of jerks, she bucked forward. Sari waved
farewell to her husband and Stevie made a face at his cousins.
Then they were off, the car snorting down New York's
streets to the Hudson River, where a ferry took them across
to New Jersey.

They went merrily south. They got lost on their way to Trenton, giving Gramp a good opportunity to demonstrate his skill at cussing. Through sheer luck, New Jersey's capital city was found amid the welter of conflicting and confusing signposts. They rolled to a stop in front of the Olde Red Lion Inn just as Lizzie's radiator boiled over. They spent the night at the Red Lion, having made a grueling seventy-five miles that first day.

The next morning was cold—even for April. Two boys from the Red Lion spent twenty minutes working on the crank before the car would start. Sari became thoroughly chilled while sitting in the car. There was no auto heater, of course, so the Innkeeper provided her with a pair of hot bricks, which at least kept her feet from falling off.

With persistence and a chunk of luck, Gramp found the Delaware River—and even located a ferryboat to take them across. Philadelphia was on the other side, but they had hardly entered the city before a tire went flat. They had no spare— it was one of those little things Ford had left off to keep the price down! The flat could mean that the tire had merely pulled away from the rim—so Gramp and Stevie hunted around to see if there were any of those new-fangled service stations with an automatic air pump. But there were none, so they dug out their hand pump from amid cans, jars, and canvas. Stevie and Gramp took turns on the pump, and both were panting before the tire was inflated enough so that they could see a rusty Philadelphia nail peeking at them through the rubber.

That meant more work. Gramp fished up the iron ham bones and wrestled the tire off the frame. Then he pulled out the inner tube and found the hole. Even harder was to find the repair kit. But after removing half the luggage, he located the kit. Then he roughed the tire rubber, coated it with glue, and plastered a patch over the hole. After that Gramp put the tub back in the tire, the tire back on the frame, the frame back on the axle, air back in the tire, and lowered the jack to put the car back on the ground. By the time the whole lengthy ritual had been completed, Gramp was so angry that he drove clear through Philadelphia and out to the Gettysburg battlefield without talking to anyone.

They spent their second night out near Gettysburg. The next day they headed for Washington, D.C.

The way to Washington was anything but enjoyable. "There were always blowouts and no gas and unpaved highways," Steve remembered, "and insects in the fields over the cooking Gramp did when we couldn't find a good place to eat." Although Stevie complained about the swarms of bugs that plagued their meals, Gramp would retort: "Hell, boy, I'd rather singe my own food than swallow the stable stews of some of those black holes called hotels."

Sari was a game young woman, but her stomach couldn't take Lizzie's unending bucking as she careened over the constant potholes that pitted the gravel highway leading to the nation's capital. She was constantly carsick that day. And when she moaned "How far to Washington?" Gramp's only remark was "Who knows? These signposts don't mean a thing they say. You'd think they were still trying to fool the rebel scouts." Unfortunately, the jesting signposts were their only indicators, for road maps did not exist.

Soon Sari's question became meaningless anyway, for from Lizzie's snout came a billowing geyser of steam. All of Gramp's tinkering and cussing couldn't fix the engine which was so overheated that it burned his finger to touch it. Except in the big cities, blacksmiths passed for car mechanics, so Gramp had to look up the local smithy. While they waited for him to muddle over the engine, Gramp, Sari, and Stevie had lunch at a nearby speakeasy. It was here, they learned, that many Washington big shots came for bootleg liquor.

To their surprise, they actually made it to Washington that evening. Their hotel room had a high ceiling with a large-limbed electric fan whirling slowly overhead. After dinner they strolled to the White House, where they leaned against the fence and gazed at the home of Woodrow Wilson.

They followed Daniel Boone's Wilderness Trail over the Appalachians. Travel in Kentucky "was pretty bad in those days," Steve recalled, "—the bad roads, the bad maps, the worse food, and the far places, but the worst was the nighttime far from a town." One night, in particular, Steve remembered, "the car ran out of gas and water, and one tire ran out of air. We stood on foot, Mamma gathering her clothes around her, and Gramp, his last match gone, chewed into the neck of a cold cigar." It was as black as engine oil around them. There were no telephones from which they could call for aid and gas stations were ten or twenty miles apart. No other vehicles were on the road at night, so they were literally on their own.

Gramp, Sari, and Stevie groped down the dark road until they spotted a huge, ghostly white farmhouse. They squeezed through a rusty barbed-wire fence—upon which Stevie snagged the seat of his pants. Hardly were they within the overgrown yard than a pack of vicious hound dogs ran toward them. Gramp frantically swung his cane at them while Sari whacked the dogs on the snout with one of her shoes. Suddenly the door of the house swung open and a man with a shotgun came toward them. Gramp fingered his moneybelt nervously. Sari's knees buckled in fright and she fell to the ground.

It could have been bad, for, after all, they were trespassing on the farmer's property. But the man was hospitable once he knew their circumstances. He and his sister treated the Longstreets to a bountiful Kentucky-style banquet. Stevie slept that night in a big bed more suitable for a prince than a Tin Lizzie vagabond.

The next morning they hunted up the nearest blacksmith. After fumbling around the motor, he said that they needed a part which would have to be sent by horse cart from a faraway warehouse. It wouldn't take long—only a couple of days. They spent the time with the farmer, his sister, and their innumerable hounds, for there was no reputable hotel within miles. Finally the auto part arrived. Then Lizzie was fixed and the three were again on the road.

Their main problem, as always, was to find comfortable places in which to spend the night. Since there were no such things as motels (the word hadn't even been coined from "motor hotel" yet), travelers had three choices. They might stay in a musty hotel dating back to the old stagecoach days. Or they might stay in a tourist home, which would be a private house with extra rooms. These tourist homes were very unprivate, with sounds coming from everywhere. For a third choice, a traveler could simply sponge on relatives.

Sick of rattletrap hotels and ramshackle tourist homes, Gramp and Sari decided to sponge off relatives in St. Louis. They remained in St. Louis longer than they wished, for Lizzie needed a new tire and, strangely, there was no dealer in this major city handling the tires of America's most popular car! After a couple of days a tire was rolled off a train from Detroit. Then they were on the dusty road once more.

Yet, for all the discomforts, Stevie enjoyed whizzing along at the breathtaking speed of thirty miles an hour. And Lizzie —she was a mechanical wonder. She chugged ever forward, taking the bumps and potholes with what seemed to be a smile on her radiator. They developed a tender feeling for the gallant machine. If Lizzie sometimes had more than her usual flat tire per day, they sympathized with her—for it wasn't Lizzie's fault that Gramp or Sari didn't see that sharp stone or horseshoe nail. If they got soaked by a sudden thunderstorm while Gramp and Stevie struggled with the canvas top—well, it was the humans, not Lizzie, who should have noticed the approaching thunderheads.

In Colorado the road became really bad. The gravel of the plains was a luxury compared with the mountain mud. Pelting rain turned the steep road into black paste. Lizzie groaned up the grades. Sometimes she gave out in low gear. Then they had to turn her around and back up the road. It was hard to see ahead and a wrong turn could have sent them tumbling into gaping ravines. But Gramp was careful and Sari prayed a lot —so they kept going.

Their biggest problem in crossing the mountains was the constant mudholes that not even Lizzie's powerful kick was equal to. Gramp was ready, however. He had purchased a thick rope and had a big hook hammered out by a bearded blacksmith at a Colorado railroad yard. Each time they became stuck, Gramp fastened the rope and hook to the front of the car, then waited for a passing horse team to pull them out. It was very slow going, and the long waits between horse teams were aggravating to a man of Gramp's volcanic temperament. But they did manage to reach Salt Lake City eventually.

After a brief stay there, they jaunted up to Butte, Montana, to see the copper mine in which Gramp had an interest. Then they were off for San Francisco. They took the forty-niners' route across the parched alkaline flats of Nevada. Lizzie's floorboards grew so hot they had to ride with their feet out of the windows, but she kept grinding out the miles. Sari sang songs in the back seat and Steve merrily plugged away at the salt-stained rocks with his trusty BB gun. Ascending the Sierra Nevada, they followed the ancient gold route around the chill blue mirror of Lake Tahoe. From there they coiled past windy peaks and cascading streams as they made their descent.

They had a difficult time locating San Francisco, for the road signs in the West were even worse than in the East. Eventually they found the Oakland Ferry. The boat trip was fun, with bay water churning about the hull, seagulls crying plaintively overhead, and, in the distance, San Francisco's skyline enveloped in wisps of fog. The air was nippy, for it was almost Christmas. Sari shivered in her big bearskin coat.

They stayed that night in the luxurious Palace Hotel, celebrating their eight-month transcontinental journey in plush comfort. The room was filled with flowers, candy boxes tied in glittering ribbons, a basket brimming with olives, and endless bunches of California grapes. After stuffing themselves, they took Lizzie on a tour of the city. The plucky car was undaunted by San Francisco's tilted streets. Although Sari turned a shade of green, Lizzie rumbled up hilly avenues almost as if she were gliding along country lanes.

The trip back East was as eventful as the trip out had been. They took the southwest route through Tucson and New Orleans. By the time they reached Virginia, Lizzie was beginning to show the effect of more than a year's constant joggling, jolting, and jarring. The car "had strange diseases now," Stevie wrote. "It moaned crossing sand roads, it balked and belched blue smoke on damp mornings, it locked wheels crossing railroad tracks, and the steering wheel froze in trolley rails. Gramp had to go out and kick the wheels free when she wouldn't steer."

They listened to Lizzie's mechanical difficulties as if they were hearing the coughing of a loved one. As they neared

Chesapeake Bay, Gramp put into words what Stevie and Sari felt in their hearts. "The old car is dying under us," he said in a voice etched with sadness.

She kept going though—a fighter even to the last. Across New Jersey she staggered—not willing to let them down. Then through New York City and Connecticut toward Massachusetts—where Stevie's father had resettled during their year and a quarter absence. But the extra mileage was too much for Lizzie. When they reached Concord, she gave her last gasp:

> One moment we were riding along, when suddenly there was a clatter of iron, a scream of tormented metal; something broke, smashed, and ground itself up under us, and the car no longer lived. We got out, steam and sparks coming from the car.

They pushed Lizzie to a side-street garage. A grimy repairman gave Lizzie a quick inspection, then grunted: "She's dead as a doornail." There was no emotion or sympathy in his voice, for he hadn't known Lizzie as a friend—hadn't seen her in her prime, when she was shiny and proud—hadn't seen her laboring up the mountains for them—hadn't seen her chugging across the deserts carrying all their luggage and never faltering in the torrid heat. Lizzie meant nothing to him.

But to Gramp, Sari, and Stevie the flivver was almost something alive. When she died, it was as if a part of them died too.

They left Lizzie in Concord and went to the train station. But as the train pulled out, they looked one last time at Lizzie. She'd always be in their memories—wherever they went—however long they lived.

That was the way Tin Lizzies were.

10

The Wizard

It was a chilly morning in 1910 and frost clung to the roof of the railroad depot. A short thin man in a long overcoat walked down the far end of the platform, away from his friends from General Motors. His head was bowed and partly covered by the overcoat's fur collar. His arms were folded across his chest, as if he were trying to hold onto something.

Billy Durant, or "The Man," as they called him in Detroit, was worried. General Motors was in desperate need of money, and to try to secure a loan he and his lieutenants were on their way to New York. Some people—many of them banking experts—openly predicted that General Motors—Durant's personal creation—was on the skids. Durant refused to admit this. He had been an optimist all his life. He lived by his wits. He wooed the goddess of luck and had managed to astound the entire business community with his spectacu-

lar successes. He had never failed in any enterprise in which
he was engaged.

Durant jammed his hands into his coat pockets. He had
always been supremely confident of his abilities. Durant
chuckled to himself. In just two years since he formed General Motors, he had deposited twenty-nine companies into
G.M.'s organizational grab bag. He had accomplished more
in these two years than most men do in a dozen lifetimes.
True, not all of his acquisitions had been profitable. But that
was no cause for bankers to call General Motors a "scrap
heap" and refuse to loan the money needed during the temporary business slow-up.

The train whistle sounded mournfully in the frosty air.
As Durant listened, a somber mood descended on him. Things
were bad, there was no denying it. Out of all the companies which comprised General Motors, few were actually
making much money at the moment. Certainly Oldsmobile
was still suffering from the lack of good management that
had resulted from the removal of Ransom Olds by the Smith
family. Oakland-Pontiac, too, was not bringing G.M. any financial bonuses. As for Buick, it was selling more cars than
Ford, but the company was so inefficient that it made hardly
any more profit on sales of $50 million in 1910 than it had on
sales of around $30 million the year before. Only Cadillac,
run by the wise Leland family, was doing well.

Despite his problems, Durant's basically sunny nature broke
through. He could not repress a smile. G.M.'s cash shortage
was almost funny. The company was so hard pressed that
whenever a dealer paid for a shipment of cars, the money was
stashed in suitcases and G.M.'s own men hurried them to the
company treasury in Detroit. This was not the way to run
one of America's foremost automotive giants. But if Durant

had allowed the money to be deposited in banks, it would be gobbled up by all those creditors whose accounts were over-due. Then G.M. would have had no money to meet its pay-roll, car production would stop, and G.M. would be out of business. It was that close.

The railroad engine pulled into the depot, steam hissing from its flanks. Durant took a seat in the passenger car. No one sat next to him, for he was The Man, and everyone knew that The Man was pondering the future of G.M. and wished to be alone.

Durant relaxed in his seat. He was a small person, so the cushions folded comfortably around him. He had always been able to sweet-talk his way out of problems. He had charm—charm to get good men to work for him, charm to get friends to put their life savings into his business ventures, charm even to make a dazzling young girl half his age fall in love with him and be come his wife.

Durant forced his thoughts away from his wife, Catherine. Yes, he had charm all right. But charm alone was not enough any longer. Bankers were iron-ribbed men. They had had enough of his wild schemes and fantastic promises. Many bankers thought that not only was G.M. about to fail, but the entire auto industry, from Ford on down, was a fad that would soon run out of gas. Durant was certain they were wrong. They would see—if he could only keep G.M. going for a few more years.

Billy Durant was in business for the sheer joy of it. He was already a millionaire owner of a huge wagon-manufac-turing concern. But he was fascinated by the limelight of power that running a nationwide business brought him. He had always been a splashy sort of person. As a youth, he had joined the Flint Conservatory of Music just so he could be the drum major and strut at the head of the parade. He didn't mind taking chances either. Like the time when, as a young man just starting out, he took orders for six hundred horse carts even though the tiny factory he had just purchased for two thousand dollars in borrowed money had only two carts on hand. He had farmed out the contract to another cart manufacturer and had thereby laid the basis for his first fortune.

Durant had not given much thought to cars at first. He, too, viewed them as noisy toys, of which the public would soon tire. But an auto ride in 1904 in the snappy little runabout produced by David Buick had won him over. Although Buick was a hot-tempered Scot impossible to like personally, he was an excellent engineer. His engine was without doubt one of the finest in the field. But he was a poor business organizer and burned up his investors' funds far quicker than they could replenish them. Indeed, almost the entire banking circle of Flint, Michigan, Buick's base, was going broke trying to support their local car maker.

Originally, Durant had no intention of becoming involved with the Buick Company. But when troubled stockholders had begged him to help get the company out of the quagmire into which David Buick had run it, Durant could not resist. Business was not drudgery to him; it was high adventure. It thrilled him to be able to make an enterprise blossom into something huge and impressive and beautiful.

He took over the Buick Company's management in November 1904. Durant quickly saw how little Dave Buick and his crew knew about creative finance. They were engineers, like Henry Ford. They could make a good car, but they had no Jim Couzens to handle the vital nontechnical angles. They thought they could run the company with capitalization of just seventy-five thousand dollars.

Buick model of 1903, built by David Buick. (GENERAL MOTORS)

Fancy finance—that was Durant's speciality. Almost as soon as he got his hands on the company, he talked the directors into authorizing a stock increase from seventy-five thousand dollars to half-a-million dollars. But the stock certificates were actually worth nothing until investors paid money for them. Other men would have had an impossible time peddling stock in a company that had barely managed to manufacture a laughable sixteen cars during the entire previous year. But Durant spoke to potential investors with crackling enthusiasm. Cars were the transportation wave of the future, he assured them. Hadn't he made a roaring success of his wagon business? Now he would do the same with Buick.

Durant's infectious charm won over Flint's moneymen. Quickly the company had its half-a-million dollars. With funds now available for full-scale expansion, Durant built six hundred cars in 1905 and sold them through the dealerships that he organized.

With that, he was in the auto race. Like Ford, Durant knew that promotion was vital in making Buick a nationally recognized car. Ford had done it by winning races. But Durant added a new twist. Not many ordinary drivers would be speeding around horsetracks. But they would all be chugging up hills. So why not promote the Buick as the champion hill climber. That decision sent Buick test drivers grinding up Eagle Rock in New Jersey. Then came the ascent of wind-seared Mount Washington in New Hampshire. Soon after, a Buick conquered mighty Pike's Peak.

As the Buick name became a family byword, Durant outdid himself by sending a driver over a snow-covered pass in South America's towering Andes. The news electrified the world.

Durant's business instincts were correct. Buick's sales shot up. By the end of 1906, Buick was selling two thousand cars. The next year this had leaped to five thousand. That was the year David Buick quit the company that had passed beyond his control and out of his understanding. Dave gladly accepted one hundred thousand dollars for his stock—stock that would be worth $10 million a decade later. Maintaining his reputation as a poor businessman, Buick lost his money in oil and real estate and spent his last years as a humble information clerk in a Detroit trade school.

By 1908, Durant was selling 8,500 Buicks, as compared with sales of 6,000 for Ford and 2,400 for Cadillac, his nearest competitors. His four-year venture into auto making had been a stupendous success. He was now a doubly rich man. But he was having too much fun to stop.

As early as 1907, Durant had toyed with the idea of uniting the major car manufacturers in one huge concern. This supercompany could bring much-needed order into the automotive business. With this in mind, Durant founded a company which he named General Motors in September 1908.

There was a little tomfoolery with G.M. right from the beginning—that was Durant's style. He incorporated General Motors with stock supposedly worth $12.5 million but actually worth nothing at all, for the company owned no buildings or equipment and was producing no automobiles. But, since The Man's name was magic among his costockholders at Buick, he easily induced them to trade their stock to General Motors in return for G.M. stock. This might seem a strange bargain, because Buick, the nation's largest auto manufacturer, was worth $3.75 million, whereas G.M. was worth almost nothing. But the idea was that the G.M. stock would pay handsome dividends from the profit of Buick, which it now owned, as well as from the other companies that it would purchase in exchange for G.M. stock.

Durant's formula worked fine for a while. As a matter of fact, with his reputation for auto wizardry, it was actually not too difficult for him to buy out other campanies. In November 1908, he assumed control of Oldsmobile by trading G.M. stock with an imaginary value of $3 million for Olds stock. Oldsmobile was a questionable company, for it had sagged badly from the days of Ransom Olds. When the stock exchange was complete, the Olds president asked Durant if he had found anything of value in the company. After Durant had examined the books, he answered: "Frankly, no." The Olds president grinned at him and retorted, "Neither have I." But Oldsmobile had a famous name and Durant felt he could bring it into the profit column as he had Buick.

Durant continued to collect companies. Pontiac was an

offhand acquisition. Oakland, as the company was known then, was small potatoes—a minor producer in Pontiac, Michigan, whose engineering and design department consisted of a single man. When Durant offered to exchange some of G.M.'s stock for Oakland's, the little company jumped at the chance.

Thus far, Durant had played a razzle-dazzle game. He had gained control of Buick, Oldsmobile, and Pontiac without paying any cash whatsoever. Cadillac was next on his list.

The Leland family, who had been in personal control of Cadillac since Ford walked out, was highly competent. Although Cadillac's sales were only about a third of Buick's, its stock brought the highest return of any major auto manufacturer. The Lelands saw no advantage in exchanging their stock for that of G.M., whose profits would be down until Durant could get Olds and Pontiac into volume sales. The Lelands, therefore, demanded 3.5 million dollars in hard cash, not G.M. stock. Durant must have gulped, for G.M. was operating pretty much without cash at the moment. But he was determined to have Cadillac. After a number of months, he approached the Lelands again. They not only refused to lower their price, but now told him that they wanted $4.1 million in cash. Durant had already decided he would pay whatever the Lelands asked. But he wanted the Lelands to sweat it out a little—maybe they'd accept a lower figure when they saw he was not jumping at it. Accordingly, Durant waited a week and a half. Then he slyly asked them if they had reconsidered. Yes, they said. Now they wanted $4.5 million.

Durant saw that he could not longer play cat and mouse with the Lelands, for it was he who had become the mouse. He got the cash by selling promissory notes secured by the assets of Cadillac. By the early summer of 1909, Cadillac was safely in the expanding web of G.M. companies. Durant kept the Lelands on running Cadillac, and a month later Cadillac accountants reported that the company had an extraordinary profit of $2 million for the fiscal year. Consequently, Durant recovered nearly half his purchase price in just thirty days.

Although Durant could feel justly elated with his acquisition of Cadillac, the necessity of repaying the promissory notes, together with the need to invest more money in plant expansion, caused G.M. to have a very serious cash shortage in 1910. Criticism of Durant's hotrod management began to surface. And there was more to it than merely G.M.'s lack of cash.

One of the most serious criticisms was that Durant had expanded so fast that he had had no time to get his accounting system straight. Parts and materials were being ordered helter-skelter by the twenty-nine companies making up G.M. and no one knew exactly how much inventory was on hand and how much on order. Indeed, the situation was so confused that Durant himself had no clear picture of just how much money G.M. owed for the goods required to keep the company manufacturing. His directors at first thought a loan of $7.5 million would get them through. Later they said perhaps $9.5 million would be better. Finally, in mid-September 1910, they concluded that, as best they could guess, G.M. would require a staggering $15 million to keep its motors running.

A few days later Durant, with an array of G.M. company presidents and their lieutenants, bought tickets for the sleeper train to New York City, America's financial center. They would go there humbly to beg for a loan.

As Durant boarded the train at Detroit on that frosty day in the autumn of 1910, he realized that the future of G.M. was no longer in his hands. Should the New York bankers refuse to grant the requested $15 million, the company would be dissolved. Probably Olds and Pontiac-Oakland would never be heard of again, and the name of General Motors would be only a footnote in automotive history.

Durant and the other G.M. officials were roughly handled by the money lords who met them in the conference room of New York's Chase National Bank. Most of the bankers were reluctant to put funds into an enterprise in such shaky condition. Durant was reminded that out of all his companies, only Buick, Cadillac, and AC Spark Plug were making money. Others, like Ranier Welch Motors, Cartercar, Marquette Auto, and Heany Lamp were drags on G.M. profits. Particularly bad was Heany Lamp, for which Durant had unwisely paid more in stock than he had for Buick and Cadillac combined. G.M. would eventually lose a staggering $12 million on the Heany fiasco. This was mainly Durant's fault, for he hadn't realized that General Electric had a more reliable claim to the patent with which Durant supposed Heany would revolutionize the electric-lamp industry.

Many of the banking group viewed G.M. as a debt-ridden monstrosity serving no purpose except for Durant's own personal glorification. Durant had managed G.M. very poorly and the company deserved to be thrown to the wolves.

Durant defended himself as best he could. He retorted that G.M.'s sales were climbing steadily upward and that its profit of $10 million the prior year should provide the bankers with more than ample encouragement for a $15 million loan. But, as the day wore on, Durant grew silent. He could tell by the bankers' stormy attitude that G.M. was through.

At six in the evening, the meeting adjourned. Durant went back to his hotel room, where he spent an uncomfortable night anticipating the bankers' rejection when they met again the following morning.

But, while Durant tossed on his bed, a conference was

going on at the Belmont Hotel which would completely alter the bankers' views.

Wilfred Leland, president of Cadillac, had been secretly summoned by the bankers. They were not quite ready to let G.M. topple, not while some of their group had suspicions that perhaps automobiles just might be more than a fad. The bankers wanted to find out from Leland why the other companies in the G.M. combine could not be managed as profitably as Cadillac. If they could, perhaps G.M. was worth the gamble.

For more than six hours the bankers quizzed Leland. With ease and directness Leland fielded their questions. At two in the morning, the bankers reached their decision.

The next morning Durant was back at the Chase National conference room. He sat down, ready for the worst. The chairman of the bankers' committee rose. To Durant's astonishment, he began speaking of the favorable future of the auto industry. In conclusion, he stated that the committee had agreed to loan G.M. $15 million. Durant's jaw dropped and he later told a friend the decision was "the surprise of my life."

The loan was a mixed blessing, however. The bankers were determined that their representatives, not Durant, should run the company. They wanted a management team that was conservative, thoughtful, and cautious, not piston-happy, mile–a–minute daredevils like Durant and his crew.

The banker management kept Durant on the Board of Directors, but he had very little authority. Then the bankers started whacking away at G.M.'s companies. Some they simply abandoned as complete wrecks. This irritated Durant, for he felt that with tune-ups and mechanical adjustments, they all could be humming once more. Even more distressing were the bankers' plans for Buick.

Buick was Durant's special baby. He had taken that company out of a tinker's garage and turned it into one of the industry's sales leaders. Durant had even anticipated Ford's secret Model T. As early as 1907 he developed (or rather experts under his orders developed, for Durant was not an engineer) Buick's first light car with a four-cylinder motor. Durant fondly called it the White Streak, since it was painted a stylish grayish white. Otherwise known as Model 10, the White Streak kept pace with the Tin Lizzie: both cars selling around eighteen thousand units in 1910. Durant was proud of his sporty little car, and with it Buick stood at the brink of the fantastic market that both Ford and Durant felt was waiting for an inexpensive, well-made car.

But the new banker managers were fearful of the unproven cheap market. Being wealthy men themselves, they envisioned automobiles gleaming with chrome and rumbling with many cylinders under a long, polished hood. Who ever heard of a car for the common man? Farmers had their horses and townsfolk could take a train or trolley or even ride a bike to

Buick White Streak, built by Billy Durant. (GENERAL MOTORS)

any place they were likely to go. If Buick entered the risky market of cheapness, the company might well fail and the bankers would never get their money back when the last and largest loan payment from G.M. fell due in five years.

So the bankers rejected the glittering opportunity that Durant had virtually put in their laps. The best-selling White Streak was dropped from production.

Durant was both astonished and enraged at the scrapping of his prized little car. He regarded it as a personal insult. It was too much for the dynamic little man to swallow. G.M. was going backwards, Durant felt, and he had no reverse gear within him. In disgust, he left his desk at the company he had founded.

To most of his business associates it seemed as if the career of William C. Durant was over.

But now there began one of the oddest sagas in automotive history. Durant vowed that he was not through. Why couldn't he recreate Buick's success with another company? He knew that he could attract the modest amount of capital needed to start a new company, for he had many wealthy friends who still believed in him. What he needed was a car to produce. Where could he find one?

Then Durant remembered a burly Frenchman whom he had hired as a driver for Buick racers. This driver had been the son of a watchmaker and knew machinery well. He had immigrated to New York, where Durant learned of him when he beat none other than Barney Oldfield in three separate races.

Now that fellow could build him the kind of car he needed. What was his name? It was Chevrolet. Louis Chevrolet.

Chevrolet was delighted to make Durant a model car. Accordingly, Durant organized a motor company in August

Louis Chevrolet in the first Chevrolet car, 1911. (GENERAL MOTORS)

1911. In order to take full advantage of Chevrolet's nation-wide reputation, Durant named the company after the Frenchman.

While Chevrolet and a few helpers constructed a prototype car in a rundown loft above a small shop, Durant and some skilled managers who had worked under him at G.M. began organizing the dealer network that would handle the Chevrolets when they were produced for the market. Durant's many friends and admirers eagerly poured money into his company and soon a factory had been rented and the machinery for mass production assembled.

Durant had in mind a car similar to Buick's discontinued

White Streak. The fact that Buick's production had plunged from thirty thousand units in 1910 to just fourteen thousand when the White Streak was dropped the following year indicated that a large number of buyers were waiting for a new model to take the White Streak's place. Durant intended to drive his Chevrolets into the gap left by Buick.

But Durant was disappointed with the prototype that Louis Chevrolet produced. It was a heavy automobile with a massive, expensive engine. Such a car would thrill a race driver, but would not have much appeal to a farmer chugging down rutted dirt roads. Yet with no other model ready, Durant was forced to produce Chevrolet's six-cylinder showpiece with a list price nearly three times that of Ford's Tin Lizzie. Durant managed to sell three thousand of them his first year. It was a respectable total for a new company. But it was not enough to cause either Ford or the G.M. big boys the slightest concern that Chevrolet was going to push its way into their market.

However, they should have worried. Durant had so much confidence in his unusual promotional talents that he could see beyond his paltry three thousand sales to a day in the next few years when Chevrolet would be a major factor in the industry.

Durant's imagination did not stop there. Once Chrevrolet was a power, Durant would take over G.M. At first the thought of tiny Chevrolet gaining control of such G.M. giants as Buick, Cadillac, Oldsmobile, and Pontiac was so absurd that Durant had to chuckle. It was like trying to knock off a fleet of trucks with a scooter.

But it could be done.

Durant thought it all out carefully. Then he leaned back in his chair and laughed until tears ran down his face. He could hardly wait for the moment he'd announce to the snobbish bankers that they were through.

The secret to the takeover lay in the fact that G.M. was a holding company. It gained control of companies not by buying them up completely, but merely by purchasing 51 percent of their stock. Thus, G.M. could control the assets of companies worth $160 million with an investment of just $80 million. And Durant, on his part, could take over G.M. —and with it all its member companies—by gaining control of 51 percent (or four hundred fifty thousand shares) of G.M.'s stock. Thus, for a cost of just $40 million, he could master the entire G.M. empire worth upwards of $160 million.

Now where could he lay his hands on $40 million, Durant pondered. It wasn't the kind of sum one kept in his mattress.

The key was Chevrolet.

When Durant founded Chevrolet, it had assets of barely one hundred thousand dollars—an insignificant sum relative to the $40 million he needed to control G.M. But Durant had a reputation for automotive sorcery, based on his fantastic career with Buick. The citizens of Flint, Michigan, where Durant based his operations, supported him fully, anticipating that he would relocate many G.M. plants in their town when he was again in charge of the mighty company.

In November 1911, Flint gave Durant a testimonial dinner, called "The Wizard's Banquet." Flint's most prominent and wealthy citizens gave ringing speeches in his support. A few days later Durant offered nearly $2.5 million of Chevrolet stock for sale. His backers in Flint and across America snapped it up. They knew something was in the air and they wanted to be part of it.

With $2.5 million in Chevrolet's suddenly bulging bank account, Durant began the battle. His first goal was to push Chevrolet into national prominence. His main line of attack was directed toward the inexpensive car market. While still producing the big, costly Chevrolet, Durant turned most of his energies toward a car named after his friend and business associate, William Little. The Little car was priced at a mere $650. In 1912, it sold 3,500 units. Meanwhile the big Chevrolet dropped to around 2,500.

Seeing how the lines of battle were drawn, Durant snatched the name of Chevrolet off the larger car and put it on the Little car. Louis Chevrolet was angry about this. He felt it lowered his prestige—as indeed it did. For some time he and Durant had been bickering over scores of matters, some unbelievably trivial (such as whether Chevrolet should smoke cigars, as Durant did, or cigarettes.) Now they argued violently about calling the cheap car a Chevrolet. Louis stormed at Durant "I'm getting out!" And so he quit the auto business at the very moment when the car which would bear his name was on the threshold of success. Although he enjoyed some successes upon returning to racing, when he died twenty-eight years later scarcely anyone remembered him.

Once the original Chevrolet was dropped and the Little car became the new Chevrolet, Durant's offensive rolled into high gear. By 1914, Chevrolet sales had jumped from three thousand to five thousand. Durant knew he had his tires in the doorway of the fast-expanding small-car field. Although Henry Ford dominated the market, Durant was not afraid to challenge this titan of the industry. In 1915, he decided to commit all of his talents to attacking Ford. Thus began one of the classic struggles of modern industry: Ford vs. Chevrolet.

In the Ford-Chevy competition, Ford held a tremendous initial advantage. The Model T had been on the market for nearly a decade. Hundreds of thousands of enthusiastic drivers

The famed 490 Chevrolet of 1915. (GENERAL MOTORS)

could vouch for its sturdy dependability. Ford had dealerships all over the country. There were Ford repair shops everywhere. Ford parts were cheap and easy to obtain. Ford's huge moving assembly lines and gigantic purchasing power enabled him to produce cars at a price that Durant could not hope to match.

But Durant had a bold master plan to grab a portion of Ford's market. Durant's offensive was spearheaded by the Chevy 490. As its name implied, the 490 sold for $490, which was $50 more than the Tin Lizzie. But the 490 boasted many luxury features that the Ford did not. For example, Chevys had fancy electric starters, whereas Ford buyers were still fussing with the dangerous hand cranks. The Chevys also had electric lights. Thus, while Tin Lizzie night drivers were cursing as their magneto-driven lights dimmed when they slowed for chuckholes, Chevy men, with headlights at full illumination, could rumble past, often giving playful toots on their horns.

This was Durant's method of attack: a little more luxury than Ford, at a little higher price. It worked, too, and before 1915 was over, Chevy sales were up to nearly fourteen thousand. Durant was the talk of the industry, for it was clear that Chevy's growth had only begun. People clamored to buy Chevy stock. Those lucky ones who did saw sales in 1916 reach sixty-three thousand cars. Although this was not much compared with Model T sales of six hundred thousand, it was a clear indication that Chevrolet was on the way up.

The following year, Chevy leaped to one hundred twelve thousand sales, giving it greater sales than any G.M. car except Buick (whose sales were one hundred twenty-two thousand).

Early in 1915, Durant decided he was ready for the assault on General Motors. Working in a little office over a saloon, he made his initial move, announcing that five shares of Chevrolet stock would be traded to anyone for just a single share of G.M. The bankers in charge of G.M. were unconcerned when they learned of Durant's proposal, for the idea that Chevrolet could take over the combined assets of the entire G.M. empire was simply too preposterous to think about.

But the response to Durant's offer was astounding. To those many G.M. stockholders who believed in The Man's wizardry, an exchange of one G.M. share for five of the exciting new Chevy was appealing. As the G.M. stock came rolling in, Durant was forced to take a larger office just to store them. Soon the rooms were filled with bushel baskets overflowing with G.M. stock certificates.

Still the bankers were not worried. Durant would run out of Chevy stock at the five for one rate long before he could obtain the necessary four hundred fifty thousand shares that would give him control of G.M. Durant was aware of this, of course, and when he became low on Chevy stock he simply had his board of directors authorize a new Chevy capitalization of $20 million. More stock certificates were issued to cover this capitalization. The Chevy-G.M. exchange went on.

Even so, the bankers felt no concern. Durant could not keep issuing Chevy stock forever. There must come a time when he would be forced to pay dividends on the stock. Chevrolet, even with its soaring sales, could not maintain its current dividend rate on all the new stock. The dividend rate would drop, and so too would the price of Chevy stock. Then G.M. shareholders would no longer find the exchange appealing, particularly since G.M. stock had shot up in value from $82 per share to $125.

What the bankers did not know was that Durant was attacking them on another front as well. He had made a raiding alliance with the du Pont Company, one of America's richest and most powerful corporations. Pierre du Pont, the company president, agreed to match G.M. stock purchases with Durant. Thus, while the G.M. bankers saw only the Chevy cavalry, du Pont's commandos were operating in the shadows. As du Pont bought G.M. certificates secretly, the prices began soaring. Soon G.M. broke the two hundred dollar mark. Then it blasted through three hundred dollars per share. The stock market was in an uproar. What was happening? Who was buying all the stock? When the price shot past four hundred dollars per share, it became obvious at last that Durant had a hidden ally.

Now the bankers became worried. But with the stock soon topping five hundred dollars, the bankers did not care to release the funds for quantity purchases. All they could do was hope that Durant and his ally ran out of money before they obtained the fraction of G.M. stock over 50 percent that would catapult them into power.

Durant himself was not at all certain how many shares he

had. G.M. stock was brimming from bushel baskets stacked nearly from floor to ceiling in his storerooms. Durant had set September 16, 1915, as his takeover date. At that time the G.M. Board of Directors would be meeting to determine the policies for the coming fiscal year. The evening before the meeting Durant and his aides began counting their stock.

They worked late into the night, passing each certificate from hand to hand, checking and rechecking to be sure the stock was correctly totaled. As they neared the last few baskets, the tension mounted. It would be close—very close. The baskets were almost empty when the recording clerk let out a howl. "Four hundred and fifty thousand!"

We can picture the scene, although there is no actual eyewitness account: the aides shouting as they whacked each other on the backs, someone tossing certificates into the air like confetti, Durant joining the jubilee with laughter and handshaking. Durant had ascended the heights of G.M. after being booted downhill five years earlier.

The directors meeting opened at two in the afternoon. The banking faction, led by G.M. president Charles Nash, refused to believe that Durant had control of the company. It was a poker-player's bluff, they scoffed. With that, so one story goes, Durant thrust open the conference room door and an army of Chevy aides marched in with seemingly endless baskets of certificates. When none other that Pierre du Pont made his appearance as an ally of Durant, Nash and his friends realized that they had been beaten. The impossible had come true—Chevrolet, the pygmy, controlled General Motors, the giant! Billy Durant's foot was once more on G.M.'s accelerator and the big show was on again.

11

Having a Lot of Fun

Billy Durant was beaming as he informed the directors that G.M.'s 1919 gigantic expansion program was proceeding according to schedule. Already Durant had increased G.M.'s stock from around $400 million to over $1 billion. With the money he had gained from the sale of portions of this new stock issue, Durant was buying new plants, as well as putting up the largest office building in the world as G.M.'s headquarters.

Billy was beguiling. He could charm a canary right out of a tree, one of his associates said. None of the directors could resist him. None, that is, except the burly, dark-haired president of Buick. He was tough, having grown up in the Kansas cowboy country. By the age of fourteen he had his own gun and could plug the neck of a whiskey bottle at thirty paces. The men at Buick feared and respected him. This was Walt Chrysler.

Chrysler was one of the few at G.M. who dared face Durant and battle him head to head, knuckle to knuckle. Walt felt that Durant was expanding G.M.'s operations far too rapidly. As Durant informed the directors about the car-frame factory he was planning, Chrysler's voice boomed at him: "Your plant will cost more in five years than we would pay for frames from outside manufacturers in ten years!"

Anger flushed in Durant's face. He started to say something, but Chrysler interrupted. "We can go out right now and buy frames for General Motors for every car division at a price that will save a million and a half dollars a year."

As Chrysler spoke, he knew the end had come. "I realized Billy Durant would be no more able to forgive such an affront than a prizefighter. . . . I had put myself athwart important plans of his. His head was filled with matters unrevealed and unfulfilled"—thus did Chrysler remember the incident in his lively autobiography, *Life of an American Workman.*

Chrysler stayed at G.M. for only a short while longer. One day he and Durant had a final argument. Chrysler shouted, "Billy, I'm done!" With that he stormed out of Durant's office, slamming the door with such force that Al Sloan, who would one day be head of G.M., heard it all the way down the hall. "Out of that bang," Sloan quipped, "came eventually the Chrysler Corporation."

Walt Chrysler did not go into business for himself right away. The money he received when he sold his G.M. stock left him a wealthy man, and he retired in splendor. But he was a rough and tumble sort of man, "seething with ambition," as he himself put it. Even more than pure ambition, he found that he loved to make things—big things. "There is in manufacturing," he wrote, "a creative joy that only poets are supposed to know." Life meant more to him than merely the accumulation of money; or even than the erection of great companies that so fascinated Durant. Chrysler had the urge to make cars. If they bore his name and made him famous as well as even wealthier, so much the better.

Chrysler's opportunity to reenter the automotive field came with the depression of 1920–21. This short, but severe business crisis hit many companies quite hard. General Motors was one. Durant was unable to prevent G.M. sales from falling catastrophically and he was again forced out of the corporation by creditors. Although Ford sailed along with sales increasing year by year, Willys-Overland, the third largest car manufacturer, was hit even harder than G.M. In desperation, the bankers who held a mortgage on Willys turned to Chrysler, well-known for his business skill as Buick's former president.

Big Walt saw a fine opportunity to exercise his talent by taking over operation of Willys. A further incentive was the fact (as he freely admitted) that his wife had gotten tired of having him around the house. Chrysler told the bankers that he'd get Willys out of its pickle; all they had to do was pay him a million dollars a year. After the bankers had recovered from their shock, the deal was made. Hardly had Walt taken control than he strolled into the office of the company president, John Willys. John loved a life of pleasure and had not put in the hard work hours that his job demanded. Chrysler announced to genial John that his salary was hereupon cut in half. Willys, like the bankers, took a moment to accustom himself to Big Walt's method of operation. Then Willys laughed. "I guess we've put our problems in the right man's hands," he said.

Willys' judgment was, if anything, an understatement. In only two years, Chrysler had Willys-Overland pretty well back on four wheels. Chrysler's energy and capacity were so unbounded that even while he reorganized Willys he was pouring a large part of his million dollar salary into the development of a new high-compression engine. When the engine was perfected in 1922, Chrysler decided to begin his own company. For this purpose he prepared to purchase a large plant that Willys was unloading in New Jersey. Chrysler's agent bid $5 million for the spacious factory. But the figure was too low and the factory was sold to someone else. Chrysler was irritated. Who had outbid him? he demanded of his agent. With astonishment he learned it was none other than smiling Billy Durant.

Yes, Durant was back again. Although he had been twice burned in his automotive ventures, he could not bring himself to leave the arena. He had an unquenchable itch to be in the midst of the excitement, the glitter, and even the hazards of the automotive world. He could never be one who watched great events from an overstuffed armchair. His mind was always on the move. He was "an unconventional soul," said one of his many friends, "who soared high above ordinary humanity."

It didn't matter to Durant that he was almost penniless after his ejection from General Motors. He was convinced that he could once again build a multimillion dollar auto empire. He determined to take on both G.M. and Ford—and for one glorious moment it looked as if he might succeed.

The Wizard formed Durant Motors, Inc. in January 1921. Hardly had he announced the availability of $5 million in company stock before he had offers to buy $7 million. Investors, both big and little, wanted to get in early with another possible Buick or Chevrolet. With the funds now available, Durant attracted some top men from his old G.M. crew. An expert from Chevrolet designed the Durant Four, and within weeks Durant had orders for thirty thousand of the $890 priced cars.

As production began to mount, Durant brought out the Star, an auto priced at $348, designed to take the market away from both Ford and Chevy. The Star attracted such interest that Durant had no difficulty in selling additional stock worth $45 million. With part of his money he outbid Chrysler for Willys' New Jersey plant—the largest single manufacturing building in the entire nation. Star sales boomed and eventually there were 1.5 million of the inexpensive little cars bouncing across the country.

Durant had plans to grab Buick's market, too. For this purpose, he offered the Flint, a well-designed car that promised Buick tough competition. To compete with Cadillac, he bought the Locomobile Company, one of the fine names in early auto manufacturing.

Durant seemed on his way to a dominant position once more. He even began exchanging his own stock for that of G.M.—an action which caused G.M. officials to fear a recurrence of the astonishing Chevy coup of a few years earlier.

But Durant's old weaknesses began emerging. His imagination could instantly convert facts into dreams—and dreams into action. But when the dreams were done and the initial actions completed, Durant lacked the staying power to supervise the dull, everyday operation of his business. He was like a racing car, built for spectacular bursts of speed. He was not, unfortunately, a gear-grinding truck who could carry a cargo safely between Paduca and Podunk.

Durant and his beautiful wife took several lengthy trips to Europe, during which times he turned the operation of his enterprises over to managers less capable than he. He frittered his energies on causes, like a nationwide contest to discover the best way to make Prohibition work. He put into the stock market vast sums, both his own and those of his friends. Indeed, the stock market became almost an obsession as he ignored his business to play the market for days on end. He became such a power on Wall Street that even President Hoover called on him for advice.

The Great Crash of 1929 and the fall of Durant's empire came almost simultaneously. He had moved too quickly. He was trying to compete with too many different models at the same time. He had not attracted the topflight managers he needed. He did not spend the hours necessary to oversee his total operations.

Although a few years later the indomitable little man would try once more—this time with a proposed national chain of bowling alleys—he would never again drive the highway of true success. When he died at the age of eighty-six, he and Catherine had been reduced to living on their treasury of memories—for they had scarcely a dollar to their names.

While Durant had been hurrying his fantasies into a fragile empire, Walt Chrysler had been moving forward at a more calculated pace. During the summer of 1923, Chrysler, his chief engineer, Fred Zeder, and a small group of expert mechanics began to put together the high-compression engine that they had designed. Just as Ford had done a decade and a half earlier, they lived and breathed the car to a point where it almost became a part of them. "We had dreamed about it until, as if we had been its lovers, it was work to think of anything else," Chrysler admitted.

While Zeder put the engine together, Chrysler was busy reorganizing the Maxwell Auto Company, which a group of bankers had asked him to put back on its wheels. But his heart was with Zeder. Soon the engine was ready. Chrysler couldn't wait for Zeder to make a body before testing the engine on the road. As eager as a child, Chrysler had Zeder fit the engine into a rattletrap car and off they went into the city.

They had fun running their futuristic engine. Walt Chrysler, millionaire several times over and one of America's foremost automotive experts, would draw up at a stop street in his tinny old car. Beside him, waiting for the policeman to whistle "go," would be other cars. Often the well-dressed occupants would look in hauty grandeur across at Walt in his working clothes. The ritzy driver would rev up his engine, eager to leave Walt and his junk heap in a whir of exhaust. Chrysler's face was impassive, but beneath he would be bubbling with mirth. He would keep his high-compression engine quiet, like a tiger crouching for a spring.

"It was the most fun," Chrysler recalled, "if this shabby old rusting car was halted between a couple of big ones. . . ." Hardly had the policeman's whistle sounded before Chrysler's car snarled forward. Within seconds he had whizzed past the startled cop, while behind him, "open-mouthed, our chance rivals would just be getting ready to go into second gear."

Chrysler knew he had a winner if he could create a body stylish enough to match his powerful engine. During the remainder of 1923 and early 1924, he and his experts designed a sleek, handsome body years ahead of anything General Motors, to say nothing of Ford with his now-quaint old Model T, could produce. He prepared to present the new car, called a Chrysler, at the 1924 Auto Show.

Everything depended on the show. Not only must the public reaction to the car be favorable, but so too must be the reaction of the bankers. Chrysler was absolutely dependent on them for a loan, since, as he admitted, "we had stretched our credit to the snapping point."

The show was near at hand when Chrysler got distressing news: he had been refused a space to display his car. The reason was that club rules forbade showing a car which had not been sold to the public. Walt and his staff were stunned. The company was through even before it had begun.

Suddenly Chrysler slammed his fist down and yelled for Joe Fields, his sales manager and man of action. If they were barred from the Grand Central Palace, where the Auto Show was being held, there was no rule that said they couldn't display their car somewhere else. Why not lease the entire lobby of the Hotel Commodore, he suggested to Fields, where many of the influential bankers and auto men were staying. Then they'd have to see it unless they had blinders on their eyes. Damn the cost of renting so large a lobby. It was do or die.

As Chrysler remembered it, "Joe Fields did not stop to ask any questions; he simply vanished. When he came back he fluttered a sheet of hotel stationery with some writing on it. 'Boss,' he said, 'we own the lobby.' "

Chrysler drove right into the Commodore lobby. It was an audacious act—cars in the middle of a classy hotel with potted palms and plush carpets. But his strategy worked.

> Although we were not in the show, we stole it! From morning until late at night a crowd was densely packed around us. Even before the end of that first eventful day we knew that our models were attracting more attention than was being excited by anything on display in Grand Central Palace. All our old friends of the trade came to speak to us in the lobby, to shake our hands and poke us in the ribs.
>
> "Seventy miles an hour? Is that on the level, Walt?" There were shrewd brains behind some of the eyes that were looking our new six over, inside and out. Now and then I would observe a rival manufacturer pass his fingers over the plush-covered seats, and I would know that he was adding to his mental computation upholstery at $6 a yard. They knew this car was a sensation, but what they wished

Walt Chrysler beside his 1924 Chrysler, the first produced. (CHRYS-LER CORPORATION)

to know was its retail price. A high-compression engine was something all automobile men appreciated, but, until our car had appeared, they had treated it as a racing driver's luxury that would be offered to the public far in the future. Yet here it was all ready to compete with what they had to offer. That was why they were so wild with curiosity about the Chrysler six's price. But we were keeping that a secret.

Then there came what we were waiting for, a nice, plump banker. . . .

The Chrysler six cylinder was priced to compete with Buick at $1,595. Walt got his loan and within a single year he sold thirty-two thousand cars. When in 1926, Chrysler, having taken over the Maxwell Company, sold two hundred thousand cars, it was apparent that he would soon be a force to be reckoned with in the auto industry.

Despite his successes, the cheapest of Chrysler's line, the Model 50, was having trouble competing with Dodge and Pontiac in the lower-medium price range. One of the main difficulties was that Chrysler had to buy nearly all his steel from outside sources, thus making it impossible for him to keep his prices competitive. It became clear that if he wanted to become anything more than just one of the many smallish auto manufacturers, he would have to obtain an iron foundry of his own. But no matter how many times his experts figured the cost of a foundry they could not come up with a price of less than $75 million. A figure that high was simply beyond the ability of the new corporation to borrow.

There was, however, a foundry they might be able to obtain. It was one of the largest in America. It belonged to the Dodge Corporation.

Dodge, Dodge, Dodge—the name began haunting Chrysler's board meetings. Somehow they must acquire Dodge. "Every time we gave the matter thought," Chrysler wrote, "we found our heads full of visions of the splendid plants of the Dodge brothers."

Chrysler pondered long and hard about how he could gain control of the Dodge foundries. Then he spun his web carefully. In the end, he achieved what he regarded as the crowning success of his life. Dodge, with its huge iron works and splendid sales organization that was five times larger than Chrysler's, was his without the payment of a single nickel in cash.

It was a most amazing story. Here is how it happened.

The Dodge brothers had scored great successes with their cars from the time they stopped manufacturing the major

Horace and John Dodge in the first Dodge car, 1914. (CHRYSLER
CORPORATION)

components of Ford autos in 1914. Using the vast sums of
money they had made from Ford dividends and the rise of
Ford stocks, the Dodges turned their explosive energies
toward forming one of the most dynamic sales organizations
in the auto industry. John Dodge, elder of the two brothers,
launched the Dodge car with an extravaganza party, the highlight of which came when John leaped to the top of the long
banquet table and jigged down its entire length smashing
electric light bulbs in the chandeliers with his cane.

It was a flamboyant beginning, and it seemed as if there
would be no way of stopping the Dodge boys. By 1920,
Dodge sales were second only to Ford. But in that year both

brothers died most unexpectedly of influenza. The Dodge widows tried to keep the plants at peak production. Although Dodge slipped to third behind Ford and Chevy in 1924, its sales were still a respectable two hundred thousand cars. Nevertheless, the widows did not wish to remain in a field about which they knew so little. Therefore in 1925 they sold the business to the banking firm of Dillon, Read for $146 million.

Clarence Dillon, head of the firm, quickly realized that he too lacked the experience to run the Dodge's great industrial enterprise. Accordingly, Dillon announced he wished to sell Dodge as soon as he received a responsible offer. But there were not exactly a great many companies with $150 million hanging loose to trade for Dodge. Ford and G.M. told Dillon they had no interest. Charles Nash, president of what would one day become American Motors, would have loved to acquire Dodge. But there was the matter of financing. Had Nash found the money, the modern big three car manufacturers would have included American Motors rather than Chrysler.

While Dillon dallied with Nash, Chrysler waited in the background. The first stage of his strategy was to disguise from Dillon just how much he wanted Dodge. For two years, Chrysler skillfully tantalized Dillon, letting him know he might vaguely consider Dodge if the price was right.

While Chrysler kept Dillon dangling, Dodge sales began to slip.

At last, in May 1928, Dillon could take no more. "He strode into my office and began to moan," Chrysler recalled. "Walter, bankers got no business trying to run a great big industrial enterprise. What do I know about making automobiles and selling them? That's your game. Why don't you take this Dodge business?"

The author with his mother in front of a 1928 Dodge.

With that, Chrysler knew he had the edge. As long as he appeared disinterested, it would be Dillon who must make the offer juicy.

"Clarence," Chrysler retorted, after making him wait out an agonizing full minute pause, "I haven't time to talk endlessly. You are wasting your time and you are wasting mine. Do you really want to trade? Then put your proposition down on a piece of paper. Mind, your lowest price! And don't forget: I'm not making the proposition; you are bringing it to me. So you had better make it tempting."

Hardly had Dillon left to figure out his asking price, than Chrysler called in two of his experts. He ordered them to unearth every scrap of information they could about Dodge—from newspapers and financial statements, from talking to Dodge dealers and Dodge workers, from whatever source they could discover. When they were through, they were to compile a minute analysis of Dodge. Dillon did not return for ten days, and by that time Chrysler knew as much or more about Dillon's company as did the banker himself.

As Dillon sauntered into Chrysler's office, he had no idea what Chrysler had prepared.

"We're not going to talk here," Chrysler informed Dillon even before he could seat himself.

"What?" Dillon answered in surprise.

Chrysler told the banker to get a couple of his associates who knew the facts on Dodge, and he would bring a pair of his own experts. Then, he continued, "We'll go over to the Ritz and get a couple of rooms. You may get a sore throat from talking before we've finished. But, Clarence, we'll stay in that suite until we come to a conclusion, stay until one of us says yes or no."

What followed was an ordeal that neither side had expected. Dillon was no pushover—no one who fought for wealth and power in America's bruising big money market could last if he were a patsy.

For one entire day the two men and their aides kicked around the terms. What would be the price of Dodge? How would this sum be paid? Would the current management remain? What percent of Dodge's stockholders would be required to approve the sale? It seemed as if the contract terms were endless.

A second day passed. Now the men spoke with voices that had a rasp. Still no agreement.

During the third and fourth days the battle went on. Dillon would give on one issue, then take the offensive on another. Waiters brought in coffee and sandwiches. Darkness fell and lights were turned on. Still the dickering continued. Dillon had to sell and Chrysler had to buy. But neither would give the advantage to the other, not where millions were at stake.

"We stayed there in that Ritz suite, arguing, eating, smoking, sleeping, talking, trading, until five days had gone," Chrysler wrote. "When we finished, all of us had bloodshot eyes from weariness."

At long last an agreement was hammered out. At first it would seem as if Dillon had won. For the price stood at an inflated $170 million—a full $27 million more than Dillon had paid for Dodge. In addition, Chrysler agreed to assume all of Dodge's obligations, which amounted to $55 million.

Yet, despite the large sums involved, no cash changed hands, and that was essential to Chrysler, for he was operating close to the marrow. To obtain the vast Dodge holdings Walt actually did not part with a cent. Instead, he merely issued a batch of new Chrysler stock with a book value of $170 million. Dillon and the other owners of Dodge were given this stock, which they might sell on the market or keep and participate in Chrysler dividends. As for the $55 million of Dodge obligations, this would be paid as it fell due from profits generated by Dodge sales.

The agreement was to take effect as soon as 90 percent of the Dodge stockholders agreed. Chrysler gave Dillon two months to secure this 90 percent. Meanwhile he began training some of his top men for their duties when the deal was finally consummated.

The people running Dodge were not certain the transfer would go through, for Dillon was having difficulty obtaining the 90 percent stockholder approval. Thus it was with great surprise that just before closing time on the last day of July 1928, that the Dodge employees saw squads of Chrysler men pull up before their building in big trucks. As they watched in astonishment, signs were nailed over the Dodge emblems. "Chrysler Corporation, Dodge Division," they proclaimed.

At the same time, K. T. Keller, Chrysler's ace trouble-shooter, with half a dozen stalwarts, marched through the Dodge headquarters to the office of the president. As of that moment, they told the bewildered man, he was no longer in authority. Walter Chrysler owned the entire Dodge complex.

Although Chrysler was elated that he now had the steel-making facilities of Dodge as well as the sales force that was the best in the business, the nation's experts thought he had made what might be a fatal mistake in his acquisition of Dodge. Dodge had been on the decline for many years, they said, and Chrysler had weakened his own financial position by issuing so much extra stock without the promise of additional dividends from Dodge to hold the price up.

But Walt saw it differently. The purchase of Dodge was, in his own words, "one of the soundest acts of my life." By obtaining the gigantic Dodge works, he not only had a strong entry into the middle-price-car field, but he had the facilities with which to make an entirely new car that could compete with Ford and Chevy in the low price range. Almost as soon as Dodge was his, Chrysler began production of his new, low-priced car. It was to be called Plymouth. Its success, at least initially, was almost assured by the incredible fact that Ford was no longer making cars.

Henry Ford had received many advance warnings that his prized Model T could not go on forever. From the very first, the Dodge brothers had told Henry that there were many improvements that should be put into the car. Ford had brusquely rejected the Dodges' suggestions. Later Jim Couzens had pleaded with Henry to alter the Model T to include modern innovations. Couzens, Wills, and other top Ford executives even built a demonstration car to show Henry what they had in mind. Ford had the car destroyed without even driving it. Edsel Ford, Henry's soft-spoken son, joined the group trying to get Henry to modernize the Model T. As the figurehead president of Ford Motors, Edsel managed to get his father to purchase the Lincoln Car Company in 1920. Although Edsel thereby broadened Ford Motors' base by enabling it to enter the luxury car field, Henry had no real interest in the Lincoln and continued to center his attention on his beloved Model T.

Henry and the Tin Lizzie were intertwined. To him the Model T represented the highest achievement of a lifetime. From the first day it appeared on the market, it had been a sacred thing to him, something almost holy. Although Henry reluctantly allowed the body to be modified for the sake of style and comfort, the Model T basics—the engine and chassis—remained virtually the same for two decades.

If, as the years passed, the Model T did not change, Henry did. Whereas once he had had a comradeship with his workers, now his organization had grown so huge that he knew few men by name. He rarely ventured into his cavernous plants. Whereas once he believed his workers labored for him out of respect now he grew suspicious that they were out to cheat him. He formed secret police units to keep track of malcontents. Under the rule of ex-boxer Harry Bennett, the secret police infiltrated every cranny of the Ford organization, even following employees to the washrooms to overhear their conversations. Bennett himself admitted that every fifth employee was a company spy.

Ford's activities brought him an average of five threatening letters a week. He carried a gun wherever he went. He installed a target range over his garage, where he practiced regularly with Bennett. He became almost neurotic about his personal safety and that of his family. To protect himself he hired a bodyguard of boxers and thugs and cultivated the goodwill of the Detroit crime syndicate by giving one of its leaders a profitable Ford dealership.

While Edsel Ford tried to function as president, Henry made decisions which undercut and humiliated his son. Operating from Bennett's basement office, Henry, as the majority stockholder, so harrassed his son that Edsel became tense and nervous. When he was angry, he vomited. Neither Edsel nor almost anyone else could reach Henry, who now preferred to manipulate his company from the shadows.

Henry had little time for his wife, Clara, who had once been so close to him. Clara, for her part, could never accustom herself to the fact that she was rich. She even kept darning Henry's socks, although he detested darned socks and threw them out his car window as soon as he was outside his mansion grounds.

The only person close to Ford was Harry Bennett, burly and brusque. Bennett raised lions and tigers at home and often took one or more of the ferocious beasts to work with him. Aside from Bennett and his animals, Henry was alone with his wealth, and his fears, and his obsession with the Model T.

The Tin Lizzie reached its all-time production high of over 2 million in 1923. Chevrolet with under a half million was a feeble second. In 1925, Ford sales slipped by one hundred thousand, while Chevy's rose by thirty thousand. Chevy's policy of introducing a new model each year was catching on. Particularly appealing were such improvements as automatic windshield wipers, clearly superior to the jerky operation of the Lizzies' hand-cranked ones.

As Model T sales edged downward, Ford became ever more cantankerous. An old man now of sixty-two, Ford was dismayed to find his dream car made fun of by an America that he no longer understood. He had given the nation a well-built car for a bare $295. The people should have been

Henry Ford beside his ten millionth Model T and his quadricycle.
(FORD MOTOR CO.)

grateful. He had almost single-handedly relieved the nation
of dependence on plodding horses for transportation. He had
opened the entire country to travel; had created new em-
ployment in such industries as gasoline, rubber, and steel; had
given an impetus to a much-needed program of road building.

And now they laughed at him. Now they were rejecting
the Model T.

Henry took his frustrations out on his employees. He
would fire men just because he saw them smoking. He became a petty tyrant; no one knew what he would do next: "I

Henry and Edsel Ford drive the fifteen millionth Model T, 1927.
(FORD MOTOR CO.)

1928 Chevrolet, victor in the battle with the Tin Lizzie. (GENERAL
MOTORS)

change my mind any time I want to," he boasted to Harry Bennett. Bennett himself, Henry's most trusted aide, could not escape Henry's arbitrary actions, such as the time Ford had a crew of painters descend on Bennett's house to give it a coat of paint whether Bennett wanted it or not. Jim Couzens, one of Ford's most valuable men, left the company in disgust. Another brilliant man left too. This was Bill Knudsen, who was soon snatched up by Al Sloan, head of General Motors, and who became a key figure in Chevrolet's successful offensive against the Model T.

Walt Chrysler watched the Ford decline carefully. Henry grew fearful of the big man from Kansas, and in later years accused at least one of his engineers of betraying Ford secrets to Chrysler. But Chrysler had ideas of his own that did not include industrial espionage. He knew that Ford was slipping badly. Whether Ford admitted it or not the day was fast approaching when the market so long dominated by the Model T would be open to others. Chrysler decided he would be there when the Model T folded. The desire to be ready for the demise hastened Chrysler's plans to purchase Dodge.

When Ford announced that as of mid-1927 production of the Model T would be discontinued, Chrysler was elated. He knew Ford had made almost no plans concerning the Model T's replacement. That would give him a full year to get into the low priced market without competition from Ford. Using the mighty Dodge plant, Chrysler began production of the Plymouth in 1928. Within three years the Plymouth displaced Buick as the third-best-selling car.

The meteoric rise of Plymouth was the sensation of the industry. *Time* magazine named Chrysler the businessman of the year. It was an honor he well deserved.

Chrysler was enjoying himself immensely. When he visited his automotive plants it gave him a feeling of power. When

The first Plymouth, 1928. (CHRYSLER CORPORATION)

he saw growing numbers of Chrysler cars on the streets, it gave him a feeling of accomplishment. Soon his interests broadened. How could he cap his career? he wondered. Why not build the world's tallest skyscraper? Work was begun on the soaring Chrysler Building in Manhattan. When the cloud-scraping monument was completed, Chrysler gave it to his children, just as an ordinary parent would hand over a toy.

Chrysler loved life. In his autobiography, written several years later, he wrote with a smile: "I'm having a lot of fun." Indeed, he was.

12

"Hey, This Feller's All the Way from New York!"

The age of the auto came quickly. When Fred Van de Water had been in grade school it was a major event to see a horseless carriage sputtering down a street. Only the rich owned one of the strange contraptions, and after they had chugged around town for a little bit, there was no place else to go—not unless they were foolish enough to challenge the horrible dirt roads leading into the countryside.

Only twenty years later, when Fred was a young married man with a grade-school son of his own, the entire face of transportation had altered. The experimental horseless carriages had given place to sleek, chrome-edged automobiles. Except for styling, air conditioning, and automatic transmission, these autos of the 1920s compared favorably with modern cars. They had automatic starters, electric lights, electric

197

windshield wipers, balloon tires, and high-compression engines that could easily hit seventy miles an hour.

In just twenty years, the familiar horse-drawn vehicle of Fred's childhood had virtually disappeared. Even in the countryside, farmers not only rode about in autos, but they worked the fields in gasoline tractors.

Seldom had a major invention caught on so quickly. In 1905, when Fred was just entering high school, there were hardly any cars registered in the United States. In 1915, 2.5 million persons owned cars. By 1925 the figure stood at an astounding 20 million, virtually one car for every American family.

As cars came into general use, work was started transforming the dirt roads into all-weather highways with banked curves and graded beds to let the rainwater drain off. In heavily used areas, two lane roads were broadened into four. The major state and federal through routes were assigned numbers and road signs were posted.

As traffic between cities increased, the first roadside businesses appeared. Hot-dog stands and greasy-spoon diners popped up at crossroads. Farmers opened drive-in fruit and vegetable stalls. Filling stations with real auto mechanics, rather than bumbling village blacksmiths, sprung into existence. A host of advertising signs were nailed to posts, trees, and barn sides. Rapidly the face of the countryside, at least along the major highways, was altered almost beyond recognition to a traveler of a few years earlier.

In the mid 1920s reliable autos, improved roads, and convenient gas stations and repair services suddenly opened every part of the nation to motorists. Thus was born an entirely new recreation—auto tourism. Fred Van de Water was one of the early tourists, and he left a record of his 1926 vagabonding trip in a lighthearted book entitled *The Family Flivvers to Frisco.*

The evening before Fred and Ellie Van de Water were to set out from New York City for San Francisco, they had second thoughts about the long journey. Although federal and state road building was progressing at a record level, highway travel was still considered a perilous venture into the Great Unknown:

> We were told much and read more about the fearful roads we should encounter in the Middle and Far West. . . . We were informed with much sordid detail of the perfectly awful people we should meet: of the rowdies who would infest motor camps; of the thieves who would rob us. . . . We were advised to beware of the alkaline water of the West which, our volunteer counselors said, scars the skin and does fearsome things to linings of motors and humans, alike. . . . A relative of my wife's, an old gentleman who had admired her from babyhood . . . became violent in his efforts to dissuade her. . . .

Rumors flew thick as bugs on a summer night about a land few Americans had really seen. Fred's slim young wife, Ellie, even grew so nervous that she asked him what she should do if she woke up one morning out West and found a rattlesnake on her chest.

Their doubts grew. Ellie turned to Fred and said she was glad their son, Freddie, was going with them, "because I've been thinking if—if—anything should happen, why, we could all die together."

Thus, looking on the bright side, she went peacefully to bed.

Despite all the dire predictions, Fred was determined to chance the hazards of a trip across the country. Packing up his flivver the next morning, he, Ellie, and grade-school-aged Freddie waved farewell to a group of friends watching them leave with forced smiles. The morning was cloudy, with the late spring air smelling of rain and wet earth. As they passed down familiar streets, they wondered if they would ever return. "No town ever seemed more desirable as a permanent residence than this we were leaving," Fred recalled.

Freddie rode temporarily in the front seat with his father as a reward for being good. Ellie sat in the back carefully reading directions from the *Blue Book Guide*. Most of the morning was taken with frantic alarms over items they feared they had not packed. One by one each was found amid the jumbled cargo heaped up in the back seat (most cars still had no rear trunks.) Nevertheless, each morning, as they progressed westward on a trip that would eventually take thirty-eight days, they went through the same heart-thumping routine of imagining they had left something at the previous night's camp. "It may have been because of this constant checking," Fred wrote with his usual twinkle, "that in three dozen camps we forgot but one article. This was a tent pole, only nine feet long."

They had decided not to sleep in the stuffy, time-decayed hotels that were found close to the railroad depots. Since there were not yet such things as motels, they became members of that informal club of the 1920s called the Tin Can Campers. All one had to do to join was to place an empty tin can over his radiator cap (which stuck up through the hood) and bring a tent and camping gear.

The first auto tourists had simply rolled out their tents wherever they wished. Schoolyards and farmers' fields were favorite locations. But the locals did not appreciate being left with a present of cans, bottles, waste paper, and other even less appealing debris. So the Chambers of Commerce began allocating land on the town outskirts for people to camp on.

As Fred and Ellie learned, most of these camping grounds operated on a shaky budget, for people had not yet learned just what a boon to a town overnight tourists could be. The Chamber of Commerce camps usually had public showers crowded into a slap-dab building where the wood floors always left Fred with a souvenir splinter or two. When the time came for Ellie to tend to the family wash, she would use the camp laundry shed where there was an old iron tub that had been some townsfolk's cast-off contribution. Ellie would hang her clothes to dry on a clothesline that did not break too often. The clothes dangled amid clouds of road dust. Later in the day Ellie would shake them out and press them with an iron so heavy that it took almost two hands to lift it. Once in a while Ellie encountered a camp with a genuine electric washer. It made the noise of a car stripping gears as it jiggled itself nearly off the floor. But the clothes came out pretty clean. For cooking dinner, many camps had community kitchens with stoves supplied with a bin full of sooty coal that Fred would shovel in when the fire got low.

After dinner, the Van de Waters would hear the families around them playing their phonographs, hand-wound affairs that could usually make it through two records before grinding to a stop half way through the third. Since the old 78 rpm records were expensive, as well as heavy to transport, the average music lover had only a half dozen to serenade him. Hearing the same scratchy recordings over and over got somewhat boring for Fred and Ellie, but it was better than listening to squalling babies.

When the phonograph session was over, Fred and his family would settle down to the evening serenade of dogs. "For some reason, which we never have been able to fathom," Fred wrote, "at least two-thirds of the nation's motor campers take their canine pets along with them." The dogs rode on the running boards, where they became irritable from coughing dust. At camp the dogs were tied to trees, where they barked away their frustrations at the slightest provocation.

It wasn't just the phonographs and the dogs which made a tourist camp of the 1920s a lively place. The nearby towns-folk added their little bit to the turmoil:

> Residents consider the local auto camp as a zoo of sorts. A favorite evening pastime is to walk out to the tourist park and observe whatever strange specimens have been added to its population during the last twenty-four hours. . . . Even after one has gone to bed he can hear the sightseers passing on foot and by car. They pause to survey the equipment, to comment thereon and exclaim: "Hey, Ed, look here. Gosh, this feller's all the way from New York!"

Although Ellie yearned for white sheets and blankets that didn't have burrs sticking to them, Fred and his son grew to love the camping life. It was a joy to wake up in the morning. "Bobwhites called us from our blankets, fluttering in the dew-wet meadows behind us; and in the misty woods across the railway cut, a mourning dove sobbed." Early in the trip they enjoyed breakfasts of fried eggs and bacon, whose fragrance wafted like perfume about them. Later, to save time, they did their frying in the evening and had a simple breakfast of fruit and cereal. For lunch they ate sandwiches beneath elms that towered by the roadsides. After lunch, Fred would seat himself contentedly behind the flivver steering wheel and sing loudly as he drove at the leisurely speed of 25 mph past the nation's lush heartland farms.

Fred was a happy soul, ever with a smile ready to curl the

corners of his mouth. He wore a bright flannel shirt that got progressively more faded as they drove day after day with the canvas top down. When Fred reached the Western states, he yielded to a boyhood urge and impishly purchased a ten-gallon cowboy hat. He admitted he looked like a walking mushroom in it, but he loved the wide-brimmed, high-peaked headdress, and even when locals gave him a playful "wheeuu!" he kept the monster hat on.

Fred and Ellie had had no experience with camping, so they encountered their share of unplanned incidents. Their tent, being nine feet tall, offered a nice target for high winds. The inevitable happened in Omaha at two in the morning. A wild thunderstorm tore up several tent pegs, then the tent pole cracked, and the whole soggy canvas collapsed on the startled family. Fred finally found his pants amid the darkness and confusion and crawled out. After much heaving in the windy rain, he was able to raise the tent once more and recover a grinning son and a fuming wife.

During the nights that followed, whenever the wind blew, Ellie nudged Fred and it was his duty to grab the tent pole and remain holding it until the wind quieted or until he dropped to sleep again.

But such inconveniences were looked upon as merely events that must be taken in stride. If one wanted to travel, he had to chose between a musty hotel, a dusty tourist home, or a not-too-trusty tent. The tent was the least of all the evils —or so most travelers of the 1920s felt.

Actually the newly found joy of taking to the open road far compensated for the scores of little irritants that the travelers encountered. Fred and Ellie knew they were among the first to tour across the nation and they could only marvel at how much easier they had it than their grandparents whose horse-drawn carriages and muddy roads gave them almost no opportunity for enjoyable travel. Certainly no family of the horse and buggy days would seriously think about taking a joyride across the Great Plains and over the Rockies to California. Yet the Van de Waters could do it in a little over a month with almost no major problems. Truly the automobile was one of the wonders of history.

To many of the early tourists the pleasures of flivvering caused them to adopt it as almost a way of life, at least during the balmy days of summer. Fred met a young couple in an Indiana camp who were traveling east. "They did not know exactly to where: maybe to Philadelphia; maybe on to Boston. They were just going ahead and turning whichever way the spirit moved them." Another couple had decided to spend the entire summer on the road just for the fun of it. The man had worked through a series of temporary jobs. He had cooked at a café, helped grade a highway, build a bridge, pick cherries, harvest wheat. He was part of a new breed: the itinerant laborer. "The odd job man who obtains a car," Fred was told, "can spend a summer roaming the country— thanks to the tourist camps—for two or three days' work each week, and between times can loaf or travel as he pleases." Expenses were at a minimum, for a night in a camp cost only twenty-five cents.

Ellie was not all that enchanted with camping, however. She would have preferred staying in one of the tourist cabins that they sometimes spotted. These cabins, the forerunners of motels, were hardly models of luxury. Most were tiny, Spartan affairs, with a secondhand rug thrown over a bare wood floor and a creaky bed that took up almost the entire room. These tourist cabins rented for the stiff fee of a dollar a night. But the demand was there and during the next decade there would be a tremendous upsurge in the growth of cabins and, toward the end of the 1930s, of auto courts.

As for the roads of the 1920s—well, they were still an ordeal. Federal legislators had finally gotten word that the voting public had enough of highways suitable only for mules and packhorses. The result had been the Federal Highway Act of 1921. The flury of road building that his act brought forth had the ironic effect of making the highways worse during the lengthy construction period that began in the 1920s and extended into the '30s, when most of the federal highways were paved.

The problem with the road construction of the 1920s was that the planners had no experience with the unusual problem of highway improvement, since there had been virtually none for three or four generations. As a result, they concentrated on laying cement, making no provision for a smooth flow of traffic while the work was going on. Instead they simply posted detour signs, which sent motorists bouncing off on ill-maintained county roads that might take ten rugged miles just to get around a single mile of construction. The Van de Water family found the hated detour signs everywhere as they proceeded across the Midwest. In one stretch of Iowa, there were ten detours on a single fifty-mile stretch. It seemed as if men and mules, with an occasional steam shovel, were everywhere as the nation made the effort to construct the all-weather roadways that 100 million motorist families now demanded.

All the work on the roads was not aimed at making them cement. It was considered a minor miracle if most roads could just be converted from dirt to gravel. Gravel might make a better all-weather surface than dirt, but the problem of dust remained:

Dust was prevalent [Fred found]. There can be no question about that. It penetrated the inmost layers of our cloth-

ing and almost worked its way through our skins. At times
. . . the finely divided dry gumbo smoked up as though the
entire road was on fire. Dust, however, is something all
motorists endure and we were able to find showers at most
of the auto camps.

As if the dust were not enough, the Van de Waters also had
to endure the highway bumps. Fred remarked that had it
not been for his balloon tires, he would have had to put up
the top to keep everyone from being bounced right out of
the car.

Through it all, the flivver kept chugging westward at
twenty-five miles an hour, which was as fast as the roads permitted. The Van de Waters watched in amazement as the endless bumps jarred loose nuts and bolts and washers from the
car's interior. For forty-five hundred miles bits of metal popped
out periodically. Yet the sturdy little car kept going and
didn't seem to care one way or the other whether Fred replaced its parts. So he didn't.

Of course, Fred could not help but develop a personal
feeling for his flivver:

> I feared him a little and respected him at times, but he
> always regarded me with sullen disdain and a clenched teeth
> expression. I treated him to all the varieties of gasoline in
> which this country abounds and he pounded along, equally
> noisily, on each one. I comforted him with oil, saw that his
> reluctant joints were greased every fifteen hundred miles
> and his crank case drained every seven hundred. I attended
> his batteries and poured oceans of water into his radiator,
> but he remained sour and unappreciative. . . . He took a
> cold delight in making me out a liar. If I boasted of his
> reliability in camp, sooner or later the next day, he picked
> up a nail or blew out a tire with a defiant and contrary zest.

Flat tires were a constant irritation. There was not a day during the five-week trip that at least one tire did not have to be replaced. Although spares were now on rims rather than being loose as they had been when Steve Longstreet's grandfather was cussing them out a decade earlier, jacking a car up and wrenching off a flat did not make a hot day any more pleasant.

The Federal Highway Act of 1921 set in motion a nationwide road identification system, with the odd-numbered roads running north and south and the even-numbered east and west. The posting of road signs was not completed in 1926, but the Van de Waters were lucky. During much of their trip they traveled on the nation's first completely marked transcontinental road, called the Lincoln Highway. To have an actual through route with signs all the way from New York to California was something to stir the hearts of motorists who had slaved so long over confusing guidebooks and confounding farmers' directions. The Lincoln Highway, which skirted Chicago and Omaha on its way west, made use of already existing local roads, and so it had a tendency to be good in some places and bad in others. It was constantly disrupted with detours and only the red, white, and blue markers shining bravely out of the dust gave the highway any dignity above the ordinary country road. Yet the signs were a comfort in themselves, for because of them the Van de Waters knew that Uncle Sam would not let them end up in a cow pasture, as the guidebooks sometimes had.

Fred and Ellie found all sorts of people touring the countryside. Most drivers had dozens of decals pasted to their car windows boasting of the states through which they had passed, or the natural wonders they had gaped at, or the overadvertised tourist traps where they had wasted their money. Many drivers were women traveling alone or in pairs, something rarely done when a cross-country trip meant hitching a horse to a wagon. Now the ladies could just push their foot against the starter, which was a large knob on the floor, and they were off.

There was still the problem of changing the daily flat tires. But this did not really cause difficulties. "We passed dozens of cars driven by women and suffering from flats," Fred noted. All the women had to do was to "sit still, look appealing and feminine and let chivalry take its course. . . . Always there was another car drawn up behind and the females were sitting and gurgling appreciation while some gallant man wrestled with and sweated over the ailing tire."

Some female drivers of the 1920s converted femininity into a diabolical method of cut-rate auto travel:

> There is on record in Oregon the case of a woman, a nice gray-haired, helpless-looking old lady, who drove her own battered flivver from Trenton, New Jersey, to Portland and never spent a cent. . . . When gasoline or oil gave out, she parked her car by the roadside, sat down on the running board where she would be in plain view of all beholders and surrendered to cries of grief. To the first travelers who stopped and volunteered aid, and they were usually the first travelers who came along, she confided in a despairing tone that she was bound for this, or that, or the other town, and lost her purse and had run out of gas. . . .
>
> Samaritans gave her gas and oil sufficient to carry her to the next filling station and enough money to buy more there. Then they passed on.
>
> But the old lady did not move. She sat still and began to weep all over again at the approach of the next car. To its occupants she reconfided her distress and obtained relief. Not until she had obtained all the gas and oil her car would hold, from the contributions of other travelers, did she move on. During this period she had also collected enough money

to pay for camp fees and food during the next twenty-four hours. When fuel got low again she stopped and wept some more.

During the 1920s another denizen of the road began to make his appearance. This was the traveling salesman. In earlier years his calls had been limited to railroad towns. But with the advent of the auto his range was virtually unlimited. "He's been doing real well," a salesman's wife told Fred one evening at an auto camp. "When you got a car to roll around in you can go to places you couldn't possibly reach if you depended on trains." Not only was the salesman doing well, but his customers were aided. Now village shops could have the same sales service that the city stores enjoyed. By the time the 1920s were over, traveling salesmen were driving the byways in ever increasing numbers. Because salesmen did not find it particularly enjoyable to pitch a tent and fry their grub since they traveled in the winter as well as in the summer, they spurred the market for cabins and for highway eating establishments.

Other users of the highways were making their presence felt. The 1920s did not yet have a name for those persons who walked along the roads waving their arms for a lift, but Fred simply called them "pests." Hitchhiking in the 1920s was different from later years when car cruising speeds would double over the 25 mph to 30 mph of Fred's day. When Fred was on the road, hitchhikers, who were then just learning their profession, would stand in the middle of the highway and throw up their arms with a hopeful gesture:

> If you ignore this signal and swerve past him, he calls out plaintively: "Give us a lift!"
>
> Once you have yielded to this entreaty, you are lost. Such a hiker . . . is as hard to get rid of as an ink stain. . . . He

will share your food and your tent if you permit. If your hospitality does not extend that far he will manage to bed down somewhere in your auto camp and appear, bright and expectant, when you are ready to start the following morning. He never is present, however, until all the details of camp-breaking have been completed.

Slowly during the summer of 1926 Fred, Ellie, little Freddie, and their gutsy flivver inched across America. Mile after mile slid past, but the family kept the same restless wonder as to what lay beyond the next hillcrest or around the next curve. The road, the road: it lured them with scarlet sunsets and meadowlark song. They were in a new world of land travel that had never before existed.

One day they crossed the Missouri River and entered the Great Plains, with the legendary Rocky Mountains edging it somewhere beneath the horizon:

> Beyond the Missouri, the road starts uphill so slowly that you know you are climbing only by the altitude figures beneath the eaves of the Union Pacific stations—while the green fields fade into brown and the air becomes clear and diamond bright; and all at once, one day, you lift your eyes from the road ahead and far away over the hot, tanned rangeland, peaks of amethyst and silver are faint against the ardent sky. Turn to the right through the mountains and you reach at length the glory that is Yellowstone.

The Van de Waters were surprised at the number of visitors to Yellowstone Park. Only six years earlier, a ranger told them, Yellowstone had been one of the quietest of the national parks, with just fifty thousand visitors coming by train. By the mid-1920s the trend had completely changed. By then visitors had soared to two hundred thousand—almost entirely motorists.

Both Fred and Ellie thought that roaming the park was the

The author in front of a 1935 Chrysler De Soto.

highlight of the trip. They marveled at the saffron and ochre gorge of the Yellowstone River. They peered with wonder into caldrons where hot springs bubbled and steamed. They stood at the edge of Old Faithful with the rest of the tourists to look in awe as the geyser spat high into the air at the appointed hour.

Fred and Ellie even had an adventure with a bear, who decided to make a picnic of food stored on the running-board luggage rack. Fred yelled "Down, Fido!" hopefully, but it didn't faze the bear. Then, with the bear's paw less than a foot away, Fred gunned the flivver. The frightful discord of pistons that had strained over several thousand miles of boulders, bogs, and buttes, was sufficient to send the animal lumbering off in disgust.

As interesting as the wonders of the park, were the experiences with their fellow campers. "The campers from almost every state in the Union who pitch their tents near yours are transformed into relatives," Fred wrote. "You appreciate all at once that there are pleasanter things to membership in the Union than the dubious privilege of paying taxes. In the auto camps of Yellowstone you get a faint, far-flown echo of the brotherhood that some day may be. You are an American. This is your land. These are your friends."

By the time that Fred and Ellie reached San Francisco, they had concluded that this spirit of oneness was perhaps the automobile's greatest contribution to the nation. After a motorist had crossed sectional borders, he was bound to take with him an appreciation of the customs of others. There could never again be a Civil War, a battle between the states, not when citizens in each portion of the nation remembered the kindnesses showered on them by the men and women—the storekeepers, the gas-station attendants, the waitresses—of other sections. "Gradually, it dawns upon the motorist that citizenship . . . is the faint equivalent of membership in a brotherhood," Fred noted, "the sign of which is a word of greeting and a smile. From Coast to Coast we met with scores of persons to whom we owe debts of gratitude. They became our creditors for favors done, for kindnesses shown for no other discernible reason than that they and we belonged to a fraternal society of some hundred and ten million Americans."

Long after the Van de Waters had completed their five-week trek across the United States they had a warm feeling for the journey. "To us ′America′ no longer is an abstract noun, or a familiar map of patchwork, or a flag, or a great domed building in Washington. It is something clearer and, we think, higher.

"It is the road we traveled."

Bibliography and Descriptive Notes

Adams, John. *The Adams Papers*. 4 vols. New York: Atheneum, 1964. A first-rate description of the colonial thoroughfare which ran from Boston to Philadelphia. It is by America's premier diarist. See especially Volume Two: 1771–81.

Allen, Frederick Lewis. *Only Yesterday*. New York: Harper, 1931. A valuable contribution to the literature of autos during the Roaring Twenties.

Bennett, Harry. *We Never Called Him Henry*. New York: Fawcett, 1951. A penetrating, rather critical insight into Henry Ford as he tended to deteriorate in old age. This is by his bodyguard, a tough, ex-boxer. Compare with a much more sympathetic description of a young Ford in Sorensen's book.

Chrysler, Walter. *Life of an American Workman*. New York: Dodd, Mead, 1937. An entertaining relation of Walt Chrysler's dynamic life up to the time he bought Dodge and created Plymouth.

Clymer, Floyd. *Henry's Wonderful Model T: 1908–1927*. New York: McGraw-Hill, 1955,
> and

Clymer, Floyd. *Treasury of Early American Automobiles: 1877–1925*. New York: McGraw-Hill, 1950. These are two books alive with photos and diagrams of the old cars.

Crabb, Richard. *Birth of a Giant: The Men and Incidents That*

215

Gave America the Motor Car. New York: Chilton, 1969. This is the best single volume of the motor industry's early days and its tumultuous growth.

Duryea, J. Frank. *America's First Automobile.* Springfield, Mass.: Macaulay, 1942. A rather dry book written many years after Duryea built America's first workable gasoline-driven auto. But it is definitely firsthand and there is a certain excitement in reading the words of the man who was the pioneer in U.S. auto building.

Faulkner, William. *The Reivers.* New York: Random House, 1962. A valuable relation of motor adventuring, at least in the novel's early sections.

Ford, Henry. *My Life and Work.* Garden City, N.Y.: Garden City Pub., 1922. There are some colorful accounts of Ford's early car racing and of his tinkering with horseless carriages. But most of the book tends to be moralizing on how one can be as successful as Henry.

Greeley, Horace. *An Overland Journey.* New York: Alfred A. Knopf, 1963. Two hundred and forty pages of this book describe a pre-Civil War journey across the country to California. Gives a most clear picture of what it was like to travel before the advent of paved roads.

Gustin, Lawrence R. *Billy Durant, Creator of General Motors.* Grand Rapids, Mich.: Wm. B. Erdmans, 1973. The only thorough book on the amazing Mr. Durant.

King, Charles B. *A Golden Anniversary: Personal Sidelights of America's First Automobile Race, 1895.* Chicago: Privately printed, 1945. This is a difficult-to-obtain, large-sized pamphlet with excellent pictures of the great Chicago Race by one who participated in it.

Longstreet, Stephen. *The Boy in the Model T.* New York: Simon & Schuster, 1956. An entertaining and poignant recounting of the journey this well-known author took as a young teen-ager across the country around 1919. Longstreet knows how to tell a good story.

Maxim, Hiram Percy. *Horseless Carriage Days.* New York: Harper, 1936. This is the classic account of early motoring days, written by a man with a twinkle in his eye. Maxim was in the forefront of the horeseless-carriage era.

Nevins, Allen. *Ford: The Times, the Man, the Company*. In collaboration with Frank Ernest Hill. New York: Scribner's, 1954. This is the definitive biography of Henry Ford. Written by a major historian. Light is shed also on other automotive giants. It is meant for serious readers, not for light browsing. But it is readable, lively, and highly detailed with personal incidents.

Neimeyer, Glenn A. *The Automotive Career of Ransom E. Olds*. East Lansing: Michigan State University Press, 1963. The best we have on Ransom Olds, but lacking in color and a humanistic understanding of this unusual man.

Oldsmobile Division of General Motors. *From Hellgate to Portland: The Thrilling Story of the First Transcontinental Automobile Race*. A reprint of the 1905 diaries of the participants. 1931. This forty-six page pamphlet was photocopied for me by Mrs. W. M. Earley of the Oldsmobile Company. To my knowledge it is not commonly available in libraries. It should be, though, for it is an account of a once-in-a-lifetime event. There are horrifying descriptions of the early roads and driving conditions in all the states between New York City and Portland, Oregon.

Pound, Arthur. *The Turning Wheel: The Story of General Motors through Twenty-five Years: 1908–1933*. Garden City, New York: Doubleday, 1934. A dated, but enjoyable, account of G.M.'s early days.

Rae, John B. *The American Automobile: A Brief History*. Chicago: University of Chicago Press, 1965. Next to Crabb's book, this work is the best single volume on the American motor industry. It is less detailed than Crabb but it covers more years.

Scamehorn, Howard. *The Buckeye Rovers in the Gold Rush*. Athens, Ohio: Ohio University Press, 1965. A firsthand picture of what it was like to cross the Great Plains and Far West in the days before automobiles.

Sloan, Alfred. *My Years with General Motors*. New York: Macfadden-Bartell, 1963. Dwells on the technical rather than the personal experiences of this quiet, hard-working man who became one of G.M.'s most influential presidents. The early chapters are the best.

Sorensen, Charles E., with Samuel T. Williamson. *My Forty Years with Ford*. New York: Norton, 1956. An excellent description of Henry Ford during his early days. A good balance wheel to set against Bennett's somber account of Ford in his later years.

Stapley, Ray. *The Car Owner's Handbook*. Toronto: Doubleday, 1971. For those who wish to know how an internal combustion engine works.

Tarkington, Booth. *The Magnificent Ambersons*. New York: Doubleday, 1918. The story's hero is not the Amberson family but a fictionalized early tycoon of the auto industry. Tarkington was a major author of the era, and this novel brings the dawn-days alive.

Van de Water, Frederich. *The Family Flivvers to Frisco*. New York & London: D. Appleton & Co., 1927. A personal narrative of a cross-country trek in the mid-1920s. Entertaining, well-written, and a pleasure to read; with many chuckles.

Waitley, Douglas. *Roads of Destiny*. Washington, and New York: Robert Luce, 1970. This is the only book that gives a unified history of the trails and roads that crisscrossed the nation east of the Mississippi before the advent of the auto. It tells of the Indians who made them, the explorers and traders who broadened them, the armies that bridged them, the pioneers who trudged them, and the stagecoach riders who bumped along them. The author had a lot of fun writing this book.

Index

About the Author

Douglas Waitley was born near Chicago in the late 1920s. His first recollection of a car is his father patting his brand new Hudson on the hood and calling it "Good old Hassenfeffer." Almost everyone's auto had an affectionate name in those days. And he remembers taking long trips with his family across the Great Plains in the 1930s, when the ancient dirt roads were being modernized with dusty coats of gravel.

Waitley attended Northwestern University, where he received a Master's Degree in history. His other books include *Roads of Destiny*, *Portrait of the Midwest* and *My Backyard*.